Hodder Gibson

Scottish Examination Material

HIGHER/ ADVANCED HIGHER
ENGLISH
Practical Guide to Textual Analysis

David Cockburn

Hodder Gibson

A MEMBER OF THE HODDER HEADLINE GROUP

Orders: please contact Bookpoint Ltd, 130 Milton Park, Abingdon, Oxon OX14 4SB. Telephone: (44) 01235 827720. Fax: (44) 01235 400454. Lines are open from 9.00 – 6.00, Monday to Saturday, with a 24-hour message answering service. Visit our website at www.hoddereducation.co.uk. Hodder Gibson can be contacted direct on: Tel: 0141 848 1609; Fax: 0141 889 6315; email: hoddergibson@hodder.co.uk

© David Cockburn 2002
First published in 2002 by Robert Gibson and Sons Ltd.
This edition published by
Hodder Gibson, a member of the Hodder Headline Group
2a Christie Street
Paisley PA1 1NB

Impression number   10 9 8 7 6 5 4 3 2
Year   2010 2009 2008 2007 2006 2005

Printed and bound in Great Britain by J. W. Arrowsmith Ltd., Bristol

A catalogue record for this title is available from the British Library

ISBN-10: 0-716-93246-6
ISBN-13: 978-0-716-93246-8

CONTENTS

INTRODUCTION

You are waiting with your friends at the bus-stop. Along comes a brand new vehicle sporting the bus company's latest logo. It's a *Gold Line Service*, and as the door opens you spot the announcement under the driver's computerised ticket machine. It says *Your driver for today is Alfred*. None of your friends seems to notice, but you do. You realise that the bus company hasn't spent thousands of pounds on the new livery and the drivers' announcements for no good reason — you know it's all part of a ploy to make the public want to use this particular bus company.

But you have developed your analytical skills. You know the desired effect — to promote a quality image of a company who cares about the public — but you also know how that effect is achieved. You tell your friends who listen in silent and respectful awe in the back seat. It's the connotations of the word *Gold*, you tell them. The word suggests not just money and wealth, but value and quality. And the word *line* is used mainly by American bus companies and therefore suggests modernity, and, of course, the word service implies a *service* to us, the customers, and assures us that we are at the heart of the bus company's thinking. There is more silence and admiration as your friends take in all that you have told them.

But did you notice, you add, the word choice and sentence structure of the announcement beside the driver? They hadn't noticed. You explain: note the word choice *your driver* — the word *your* suggests that there is a personal relationship between him and yourself, that he is, if you like, your own chauffeur, and that you belong to the company and it to you. What about the sentence structure, one of your friends quizzes; he tells you that he never knows what to say when asked to comment on sentence structure.

You smile. Imagine, you elucidate, that the sentence had been in the passive voice, that it said instead *This bus is driven by Alfred*. I see, said the friend who had been frowning, a look of enlightenment suffusing his entire face. That's more formal, much less personal, he comments. And the very fact that the driver is named, that's a kind of word choice too. You sit back in your seat to enjoy the rest of the journey in the certain knowledge that you have explained to them all that Textual Analysis entails.

Textual Analysis is not just an important part of Higher English. Textual Analysis is the basis for an entire approach to literature. When you set out to read a book — or watch a film — you are entering a world of imaginative fiction. The author — or director — has deliberately created a story that is intended to engage your interest, that will entertain you, and that will perhaps reveal something to you about the nature of human existence.

You and I as intelligent readers — or viewers — should be able to examine the book — or film — critically, so that we can say what our considered opinion of it is and whether or not we think that it is any good. When we read a novel or poem or see a play, we know what our reaction is, we know whether it bores us or entertains us or saddens us or makes us laugh, and we trust that initial and vitally important gut response. In other words, we know the effect, but we need to know how that effect has been achieved, just as the group getting on the bus found out how the bus company had used language to achieve the desired effect among its customers.

Textual Analysis is a set of skills that will help you understand a text, come to terms with it, and be able to write about it meaningfully. It will help you with all aspects of your English course. It will also help you to understand the world of advertising, the world of marketing, and give you a critical insight into the plethora of images, both verbal and visual, with which we are bombarded daily. Above all, it will teach you about the importance of the effects of language.

In fact, it is the proper approach to the study of all English literature.

CHAPTER ONE

What is textual analysis about?

You know what it is like when you watch a video with your friends. After it is finished you must have experienced the business of talking about it. One of you thinks that it was great, but someone else disagrees: then you start discussing what was good about it and what was not. Someone points out that one of the characters was a real "baddie", while another friend points out that the same character had some good points, that there was an explanation for his motives.

Such a discussion, believe it or not, is a form of analysis! Not only that, but it is not that far removed from what we have come to call textual analysis — you are examining the text and interpreting it while at the same time making comments about the ways in which the text has been put together. A "text", I should point out, does not have to be a literary text, but can be anything that is written or, indeed, anything that is viewed, such as a video.

Our business, as far as the purpose of this book is concerned, however, is the examination of written texts.

To make that easier for you, there are three questions that will help you deal with textual criticism. Whenever you read a text, I want you to think of these three questions and the ways in which you should go about answering them.

The first question that I want you to consider after you have read the poem or the play or the novel or the extract is:

    (a) What is the passage / poem / extract about?

And then the related question to find out what the effects of the piece are and how we, as the reader (viewer), react to these effects:

    (b) What effects does the piece have on me?

Then, in order to find out how the writer has achieved these effects, we have to ask ourselves a third question:

    (c) How have these effects been achieved?

This last question gets at the very heart of textual analysis.

When next your teacher, after having read you an extract, asks for your opinion, bear these questions in mind: they'll go a long way towards helping you to form your reply.

Let's take a fairly straightforward example of what I mean and see how these questions work out in practice. I want you to read the following passage carefully:

The extract is taken from the first part of an essay called *The Passing Wisdom of Birds* by Barry Lopez. It deals with the arrival of the Spanish soldier Cortés and his men in Tenochtitlán (Mexico City) in 1519. The extract begins with the author's speculations on the thoughts of the Spanish invaders as they approach Tenochtitlán.

THE PASSING WISDOM OF BIRDS

It is impossible to know what was in the facile, highly charged mind of Cortés that morning, anticipating his first meeting with the reluctant Montezuma; but Bernard Diaz, who was present, tells us what was on the minds of the soldiers. They asked each other was it real — gleaming Iztapalapa behind them, the
5 smooth causeway beneath their feet, imposing Tenochtitlán ahead? The Spanish had been in the New World for twenty-seven years, but what they discovered in the Valley of Mexico that fall "had never been heard of or seen before, not even dreamed about" in their world. What astounded them was not, solely, the extent and sophistication of the engineering that divided and
10 encompassed the lakes surrounding Tenochtitlán; nor the evidence that a separate culture, utterly different from their own, pursued a complex life in this huge city. It was the depth and pervasiveness of the natural beauty before their senses.

The day before, they had strolled the spotless streets of Iztapalapa through plots
15 of full-blossomed flowers, arranged in patterns and in colours pleasing to the eye; through irrigated fruit orchards; and into still groves of aromatic trees, like cedar. They sat in the shade of bright cotton awnings in quiet stone patios and marvelled at the robustness and well-tended orderliness of the vegetable gardens around them. Roses glowed against the lime-washed walls of the
20 houses like garnets and alexandrites. In the hour before sunset, the cool, fragrant air was filled with the whirr and flutter of birds, and lit with birdsong.

That had been Iztapalapa. Mexico City, they thought, even as their leader dismounted that morning with solemn deliberation from that magical creature, the horse, to meet an advancing Montezuma ornately caparisoned in gold and
25 silver and bird feathers —Mexico City, they thought as they approached, could only outdo Iztapalapa. And it did. With Montezuma's tentative welcome they were free to wander in its various precincts. Mexico City confirmed the image of a people gardening with meticulous care and with exquisite attention to line and detail at the edge of nature.

30 It is clear from Diaz's historical account that the soldiers were stunned by the physical beauty of Tenochtitlán. Venice came to their minds in comparison, because of its canals; but Venice was not as intensely fresh, as well lit as Mexico City. And there was not to be found in Venice, or in Salamanca, or in Paris for that matter, anything like the great aviaries where thousands of birds — white

35   egrets, energetic wrens and thrushes, fierce accipiters, brilliantly coloured parrots — were housed and tended. They were as captivating, as fabulous, as the displays of flowers; vermilion flycatchers, copper-tailed trogons, green jays, blue-throated hummingbirds, and summer tanagers. Great blue herons, brooding condors.

40   And throughout the city wild birds nested.

    Even Cortés, intensely preoccupied with politics, with guiding a diplomacy of conquest in the region, noticed the birds. He was struck, too, by the affinity of the Mexican people for their gardens and for the measured and intricate flow of water through their city. He took time to write Charles V in Spain, describing it
45   all.

    Cortés's men, says Diaz, never seemed to tire of the arboretums, gardens, and aviaries in the months following their entry into the city. By June 1520, however, Cortés's psychological manipulation of Montezuma, and a concomitant arrogance, greed, and disrespect on the part of the Spanish military force had
50   become too much for the Mexicans, and they drove them out. Cortés, relentless and vengeful, returned to the Valley of Mexico eleven months later with a larger army and laid siege to the city. Canal by canal, garden by garden, home by home, he destroyed what he had described to Charles V as "the most beautiful city in the world". On June 16, in a move calculated to humiliate and frighten the
55   Mexican people, Cortés set fire to the aviaries.

Barry Lopez

Let's begin with the first question: *What is the passage about?* This question isn't asking you to retell the plot. There is no point in doing that since, no matter how talented you are, you are unlikely to be able to improve on the way that the author relates the story. In any case, you know from experience that those people who try to retell the plot of some film or TV programme that they've recently seen tend to be the biggest bores on the planet. Since you want to avoid being thought of as tedious, avoid retelling plots. What is the question getting at then? The question is asking about the theme or issue that the writer is dealing with; or rather, the question is asking what issues you — as the reader — think that the writer is dealing with.

You've read the extract — so, now, answer the question: *What issues do you think Barry Lopez is getting at?* Your answer, I hasten to add, has to be based on the text itself: you can't just launch off into the realms of fantasy and say that you think he was dealing with, say, animal rights because the birds in the extract were horribly abused. You have to be sensible. Read it carefully, then, basing your answer on the text, say what issues strike you most forcibly. You need to be able to defend your answer by returning to the text to prove your case.

You might give a variety of responses to this question: it is about "injustice", you think. Or perhaps "inhumanity". Maybe the "cruelty and evil of imperialism". Maybe you think it is simply about "revenge". You may even think of some other issue right now that I haven't thought of, and if you can, that's all to the good. Whatever you — or we — think it is about, the important matter is that we can justify our claim by reference to the text.

Let's assume that we think it is about revenge. Does the text support such a claim? Go back to what the author wrote and you will read in the paragraph beginning on line 46 the sentences "By June 1520, however, Cortés's psychological manipulation . . . and laid siege to the city." In these sentences, the author makes clear the reason for the Mexican's driving out the Spaniards and then words such as "relentless" and "vengeful" suggest very powerfully that when Cortéz later returned to Mexico City his siege was motivated by revenge.

Are you getting the idea? Let's take another of the issues that we thought it might be about: inhumanity. That's easy, you tell me, the evidence is once again in the same paragraph where the author states "in a move calculated to humiliate and frighten the Mexican people, Cortés set fire to the aviaries". I agree, but there is further evidence of inhumanity elsewhere in the extract: can you find it? You will by now have gathered that this is the question which relates to **understanding**.

We now know *how* to answer the first of our three questions:

What is the passage about?

What of question *(b), What effect does the piece have on me?* This is the question which relates to **personal reaction**. How to answer this question is the subject of the next chapter.

But let me say a bit more about the answer to question *(a): What is the passage about?* You might be heartened to know that really there are only three themes in literature — birth, marriage, and death.

By birth I do not simply mean themes about being born — though that is important and actual birth appears in many texts — but I also mean the kind of questions that arise as a result of being born. Questions such as 'Why am I here?", "What about my future?", "What is life about?" These are questions which are asked by the young — people such as yourself. You have your entire life ahead of you and it's only natural that you will ask yourself questions such as "What will become of me?" Many texts deal with such questions — questions about the nature of life and existence.

By marriage, I mean both the traditional husband and wife relationship, but I also interpret marriage in a much wider sense to encompass all relationships — relationships with parents, with friends, with members of the opposite sex, with authority figures, etcetera. Under relationships come themes such as jealousy, betrayal, revenge, unrequited love, treachery, loyalty, trust . . .

Finally, by death, I don't just mean the process and act of dying — though death itself is an important theme in many texts — but also the questions upon which impending death causes us to reflect: questions such as "Why was I here?" "What have I done with my life?", "What do I do with the years that remain?", "What has it all been about?" These are questions that do not — cannot — much trouble the young, though they are questions that can plague the middle aged and elderly, like flies about our heads.

I have to say, of course, that although question *(a) What is the passage about?* is the first question we ask, the answer to it will emerge with greater and greater clarity once we have answered the other two questions and after we have studied the text in more and more detail.

A final word on the subject of themes or issues. Some people claim that themes and issues have to do with what the author intended, but I want to dispel such an approach to textual analysis. It does not matter what the author intended or intends: in the case of dead authors, intent is irrelevant since we can hardly phone up Shakespeare and ask him what he had in mind when he wrote *Hamlet*. I am going further than that, however: I am saying that even if you could phone up Shakespeare — or Edwin Morgan — and ask either of them what they *meant* by a given text, their answer may be interesting, but it cannot interfere with the meaning that you or I or any individual reader derives from the text. The theme — or meaning — of a text is a function of the reading process.

CHAPTER TWO

What effects does the piece have on me?

In answering this question, you need to be aware of the effects that have been created as well as your emotional reaction to the effects. In other words, this question involves both intellectual comprehension and your emotional reaction.

What do I mean by "emotional reaction"? Think again of a film or video that you have seen recently and thoroughly enjoyed. You recommend it to your friends: "You must see *such-and-such*, it's great," you tell them. You recommend the film because of how you felt while you were watching it. Now try to remember exactly how you did feel while you were watching it. Did it make you cry? Or laugh? Or feel sad? Or did it have you on the edge of your seat with excitement? Did it scare you? Make you feel frightened? That's what I mean by "emotional reaction" – what you actually *felt* while watching.

There is, of course, another response which is just as important: have you ever watched a film or video — often one that's been recommended by a friend — where half way through you get up to make a cup of tea or take the dog out for a walk? Have you ever sat in the cinema or the theatre — from which escape is more difficult — and felt an uncomfortable and increasing numbness in that part of the anatomy that's at the opposite end from the brain? We are talking about boredom. Sometimes our reaction to a film is simply one of wanting to leave the cinema or switch off the video recorder, and that is as valid a reaction as any other.

What I have said about films is just as true about books and plays and poems. We react to them as well, and we have to learn to trust those reactions. Really, if you think about it, authors and film directors don't create "works of art" just so that generations of Fifth Year pupils can have their lives made miserable by having to answer exam questions about them. Such people write books and direct movies in order that the audience does laugh or cry or feel scared or sad or excited or whatever. It's your personal response that matters.

When it comes to the written texts, however, I have to say a word about boredom. I said that it is a perfectly valid reaction, and that is true. But we have to ask ourselves why we are bored by a book. I think that the answer may be a complex one that has to do with the reasons why we read books in the first place.

When we read a novel or a poem or when we go to the theatre to see a play we do so for two main reasons: either to confirm our experience or to extend it. Most probably, it is a combination of both reasons. By its very nature, experience — the kinds of things we go through in our normal day-to-day living — is private, swarming, unpredictable and chaotic. It is private in that what we feel cannot be shared with any other human being except through language.

When I feel sad, there is really no way that I can *know* that what I feel is the same thing as you feel when you are sad, except by means of language. We can talk about our feelings. But the point is that we cannot know that we are actually feeling exactly the same feeling.

By chaotic, I mean that things happen to us, in the hurly-burly of daily life, so fast and so haphazardly that we find it difficult to find time to sort out our experiences in such a way that we can make sense of them. We may talk about them with our friends or parents, and while that may help, it doesn't always clarify what the day has done to us or what it is that we are feeling.

An author is a person who feels his / her experiences more keenly than the rest of us, and who is further possessed of the linguistic skills to re-create those experiences in words, in the same way as an artist might create them in paint or a musician using musical notation. The novelist is someone who has the skill to put his / her experiences into words with great clarity. Now if the novelist is dealing with experiences that we have already had or are going through, then we read his work avidly, precisely because it achieves what we have neither the time nor the skill to manage: a clarification of our own experience. We bring our private and chaotic experience to the novel, where it is sorted out, re-patterned, made clearer.

That almost makes the novel out to be some kind of emotional therapy — and maybe it is — but it might explain why we can get so involved in a story that deals with the very things we are going through.

Of course it may be that we read, not to get even more involved with our experience, but to escape the very chaos of it: we may want to get involved in a story that takes us out of ourselves, away from the problems that life seems to present. That, too, is a valid reason for reading.

As I said, I suspect that we read for a combination of both these reasons. But, and this is where boredom might set in, if the book deals with experiences that are alien to us in such a way that we can neither identify with nor escape into, then we become bored. We may be bored by *Macbeth* simply because we find it difficult to identify with a tyrannical man who seems to derive so much pleasure in carving people up and making their lives unbearably miserable. On the other hand, we may be bored by a book such as *Z for Zacharia* because the experiences it deals with are too trivial to capture our interest. That is not to say that it is a bad or inferior novel; merely that we have outgrown its concerns.

The effect that any literary work has on us, then, is clearly related to our level of maturity. As we grow older we become more demanding: our taste develops and becomes more discriminating.

There is, of course, another factor involved when we read books: our imagination. Although we may not have gone through certain experiences, that doesn't mean to say that we cannot imagine them. I am not a eighty-year-old man who has given away his kingdom to ungrateful daughters and has consequently been driven to the point of madness, but that doesn't stop me either enjoying or understanding *King Lear*. I can enter imaginatively into Lear's world and engender great sympathy for his plight: the power of the story combines with the power of my imagination to create the very emotional response that I am talking about, even although I have no direct experience of the situation in which the characters find themselves.

The point I am trying to make is that, when you are reading a piece of literature, you should pay attention to your emotional reaction. Bring your own experience to what the novelist or poet or playwright says and allow the text to be illuminated by that experience and, in turn, to illuminate your experiences.

Of course, it is very often the case that our own experiences are illuminated by the text. Sometimes you even stop reading, stunned by some particular point in the story, to reflect that it captures exactly how you felt last Tuesday. Then you really have been captured by the power of literature.

So far I have been talking about the general effect a story has on you personally. But it is also important to be able to reflect on particular aspects of that story, such as its beginning or the ending or some striking bit between. The beginning of a story has to establish what we call "mood" or "atmosphere" and these words often defeat candidates because they are uncertain of their meaning. Yet the mood or atmosphere of a text is very important in terms of how we relate personally to the work.

I can best explain what I mean by referring once again to films. At the very beginning of a movie, the director has to establish for the audience what kind of film it is going to be about. If it is a very sad story that he / she wants to depict, then he's hardly likely to begin it with shots of a cobalty blue Mediterranean sea lapping lazily onto some sparkly sun-soaked sands where groups of holidaymakers are happily and playfully bathing. He is much more likely to use a setting that is dismally grey and windswept with rain. The director wants to establish the right "atmosphere".

It's the same with a novelist: he / she will open the novel by creating the right kind of atmosphere by using an appropriate setting and appropriate words. Although the Barry Lopez extract is not from a novel, you'll easily see what I mean. Let's look at the second paragraph:

> The day before, they had strolled the spotless streets of Iztapalapa through plots of full-blossomed flowers, arranged in patterns and in colours pleasing to the eye; through irrigated fruit orchards; and into still groves of aromatic trees, like cedar. They sat in the shade of bright cotton awnings in quiet stone patios and marvelled at the robustness and well-tended orderliness of the vegetable gardens around them. Roses glowed against the lime-washed walls of the houses like garnets and alexandrites. In the hour before sunset, the cool, fragrant air was filled with the whirr and flutter of birds, and lit with birdsong.

Here, the author is establishing mood or atmosphere. The setting has already been established — the Valley of Mexico, but he is now going into more detail about Iztapalapa. He is dealing with setting, but there are certain words which also establish atmosphere: *strolled the streets, full-blossomed flowers, colours pleasing to the eye, aromatic trees, bright cotton awnings*. What atmosphere do these words conjure up? Happiness? Lack of threat — from *strolling*? Attractiveness? Sun? Fragrant smells? It is altogether a pleasant, sunny, clearly foreign place, and we know that from the words that the author uses — a term we call *word choice*.

The reader gets the impression that nothing could go wrong — and, of course, that is deliberate in order to create a powerful contrast with the horror that is still to come.

You will find, more often than not, that the first question in the textual analysis section will ask you about the mood or atmosphere that is established. Now you know how to set about answering it. And remember we are dealing with our own *personal* reaction — how we react to the words used. It is our own experience of pleasing colours and aromatic trees that help us determine the mood of this particular text.

Now that you know how best to answer Question 2 — *What effects does this piece have on me?* — we can go on in the next chapter to answer the third question — *(b) How have these effects been achieved?* The answer to this question has to do with **analysis** and **evaluation**.

CHAPTER THREE

How have these effects been created?

This question goes to the heart of textual analysis. Let's begin by examining words and the contexts in which we use them. Before we answer the question, *How have these effects been created?*, we need to examine carefully the different levels of meaning that words can have, and we need to examine how meaning is derived from context.

Take, for example, the word "school". We all know what it means, but that meaning can vary according to the context in which the word is used. The context helps to define the exact meaning that the author or speaker intends. The word "school" means one thing when the context is education:

> *At the school I go to, the teachers are very good.*

The meaning of the word — a building where young people are educated — is established by the context: the idea of its being somewhere I go to and by the word "teachers". But take the sentence:

> *A dolphin is a social animal that travels around in a school.*

Here the different context gives the word a different meaning. In this sentence "school" doesn't mean a building dedicated to the teaching of the young, but means a group — in this case of marine cetacean mammals. Think how the word "pride" can change its meaning quite dramatically from "Pride goes before a fall" to "A pride of lions".

Context, then, is a vital clue to the meaning of a word. Indeed, when we come across an unfamiliar word, we can often work out its meaning from the context in which it is used. Sometimes in the interpretation paper you are asked to derive the meaning of a word from its context and to show how that context helped you arrive at the meaning — now you know how to answer that question!

What we are talking about at the moment is the *denotative* or dictionary meaning of words. The word "school" means a building where young people are educated in the sentence:

> *At the school I go to, the teachers are very good.*

That is, given the context, if we looked up the word "school" in the dictionary, we would find that kind of meaning — the denotative meaning, what the word denotes. Words after all stand for — or denote — things or objects. That must have been how language started: instead of having to grunt and point, primitive people found that life was easier if the thing being grunted at and pointed to had a name.

But the notion of meaning is a bit more complex than this suggests. Words don't just stand for things, words also have associations. To put it technically, words don't just have denotative meaning, they also have connotative meaning. That is what I meant when I said in the opening sentence of this chapter that we had to look at the different levels of meaning.

The connotative meaning of a word is the association that the word has for you, your experience of the word, and what comes into your head when you hear it. For example, to take the word "school" again, the association of that word for someone who has been entirely successful within the institution will be quite different from the association it has for someone who has spent most of his time in trouble there.

The connotative meaning — or connotation — of a word is the association that the word has for us, the mental picture that it conjures up, the feelings that the word creates in us. When it comes to textual analysis, it is vital that we are aware of this level of meaning. An author certainly is, and he / she will exploit it to the full to create the desired effect.

Words, then, have denotative meaning — where they represent things; and connotative meaning — where they suggest things. Both meanings are circumscribed — limited and defined — by the context in which they appear. For example, look at the sentence:

Darren went up to the bar and bought a drink.

The words "Darren", "bar", and "drink" can have all kinds of denotative and connotative meanings but, brought together the way they are in this sentence, a context is created where each word works on the other limiting and defining its meaning. We know that the bar which Darren approaches isn't the bar in a gym or a chocolate bar because the word "drink" prevents the possibility of those meanings, and we know that the drink referred to isn't a synonym for the sea because Darren bought it in a bar. We can't just let our imaginations run riot when we see a word — we must pay attention to the context, which will limit the possibilities of meaning for us.

So far, we talked only about words and their meaning. But words are used in *sentences* and sentences themselves have meaning. Sometimes that meaning is *literal* and sometimes it is *metaphorical*. In the sentence below —

> *Darren went up to the bar and bought a drink.*

— the meaning is quite literal: Darren went up to a real bar and bought a real drink. But take the sentence:

> *Darren went up to the bar and took the biscuit.*

Now the sentence might be literally true — there might have been a real biscuit that Darren took and gobbled with his diet Coke. But more likely the sentence is metaphorically true: Darren said something cheeky to the bar staff that had them speechless with outrage. Examine the following lines from *Hamlet* (end of Act III, scene ii):

> *'Tis now the very witching time of night,*
> *When churchyards yawn, and hell itself breathes out*
> *Contagion to this world. Now could I drink hot blood . . .*

Shakespeare is employing metaphorical language here: it isn't literally true that churchyards "yawn", or that hell "breathes out" vile diseases on the world, nor does Hamlet intend to have a night-cap of warm blood. These are metaphors, but look carefully how these metaphors are linked by the ideas of yawning, breathing and drinking.

Sometimes the language can be both literally and metaphorically true. Let's look at other lines from *Hamlet*, this time from earlier in the play. Hamlet and Ophelia, in what is called the Nunnery Scene, are quarrelling, among other things, about love letters that Hamlet had previously given her. In this scene, Ophelia is returning these letters to Hamlet, who denies having sent them in the first place. Ophelia claims that he did send the letters:

> *My honoured lord, you know right well you did,*
> *And with them words of so sweet breath composed*
> *As made these things more rich. Their perfume lost,*
> *Take these again, for to the noble mind*
> *Rich gifts wax poor when givers prove unkind.*

Their perfume lost, to me as a reader, is both literal and metaphorical: Hamlet no doubt had used scented paper, but Ophelia is also referring to their content which to her was so beautiful that it was like perfume. Other words such as "so sweet breath composed" and "made these things so rich" suggest the beauty of the content and therefore help us spot the metaphor in *Their perfume lost*.

At any rate, the line is ambiguous — it can be read either literally or metaphorically or as both — and that is another device employed by authors for effect: ambiguity.

In case you think that I have forgotten all about the Barry Lopez extract, let's go back to it and look at lines 20–21:

> *In the hour before sunset, the cool, fragrant air was filled*
> *with the whirr and flutter of birds, and lit with birdsong.*

The author is clearly exploiting a mixture of senses which creates a powerful, sensual reaction in the reader. The words *lit* and *birdsong* refer to different senses: *lit* has to do with our sense of sight and *birdsong* has to do with our sense of hearing. And this mixed appeal to our senses draws attention to the richness of the atmosphere. But there is also a metaphor lurking about. The use of the word *lit* in this context also suggests *illuminate* in the sense that the sound shed light on or illuminated the feelings that the men had while walking.

Don't worry about the idea of metaphor — you will find out more about this device in a later chapter.

To recap: we've looked at the denotative and connotative meanings of words, the importance of context, the use of metaphorical language, and the use of ambiguity.

We have, however, only scratched the surface of the question, *How have these effects been achieved?* As I said previously, this question penetrates the very heart of textual analysis, and we need, therefore, to devote several chapters to answering it properly. We need to examine Narrative Structure, Sentence Structure, Situation, Word Choice, Mood, Literary Devices, Rhythm, and Sound.

The following chapters will deal with each of these topics in turn.

CHAPTER FOUR

Structure

Of these aspects of textual analysis — Narrative Structure, Sentence Structure, Situation, Word Choice, Mood, Literary Devices, Rhythm, and Sound — we will begin with Structure.

The word *structure* usually renders most candidates paroxysmic with dread. In textual analysis — and in the interpretation paper — you can be asked about the structure of a sentence, or of a paragraph, or, indeed, of the whole passage or poem. And, you'll be comforted to know, the ideas that lie behind the word *structure* are not at all difficult. You will find it all quite straightforward.

But first of all I want you to read this longish passage, called *A Hanging*, by George Orwell. I think that you will find the piece quite interesting.

A HANGING

1   It was in Burma, a sodden morning of the rains. A sickly light, like yellow tinfoil, was slanting over the high walls into the jail yard. We were waiting outside the condemned cells, a row of sheds fronted with double bars, like small animal cages. Each cell measured about ten feet by ten and was quite bare within except for a plank bed and a pot of drinking water. In some of them brown silent men were squatting at the inner bars, with their blankets draped round them. These were the condemned men, due to be hanged within the next week or two.

2   One prisoner had been brought out of his cell. He was a Hindu, a puny wisp of a man, with a shaven head and vague liquid eyes. He had a thick, sprouting moustache of a comic man on the films. Six tall Indian warders were guarding him and getting him ready for the gallows. Two of them stood by with rifles and fixed bayonets, while the others handcuffed him, passed a chain through his handcuffs and fixed it to their belts, and lashed his arms tight to his sides. They crowded very close about him, with their hands always on him in a careful, caressing grip, as though all the while feeling him to make sure he was there. It was like men handling a fish which is still alive and may jump back into the water. But he stood quite unresisting, yielding his arms limply to the ropes, as though he hardly noticed what was happening.

3   Eight o'clock struck and a bugle call, desolately thin in the wet air, floated from the distant barracks. The superintendent of the jail, who was standing apart from the rest of us, moodily prodding the gravel with his stick, raised his head at the sound. He was an army doctor, with a grey toothbrush moustache and a gruff voice. "For God's sake hurry up, Francis", he said irritably. "The man ought to have been dead by this time. Aren't you ready yet?"

4   Francis, the head jailer, a fat Dravidian in a white drill suit and gold spectacles, waved his black hand. "Yes sir, yes sir", he bubbled. "All iss satisfactorily prepared. The hangman iss waiting. We shall proceed."

5   "Well, quick march, then. The prisoners can't get their breakfast till this job's over."

6   We set out for the gallows. Two warders marched on either side of the prisoner, with their rifles at the slope; two others marched close against him, gripping him by arm and shoulder, as though at once pushing and supporting him. The rest of us, magistrates and the like, followed behind. Suddenly, when we had gone ten yards, the procession stopped short without any order or warning. A dreadful thing had happened — a dog, come goodness knows whence, had appeared in the yard. It came bounding among us with a loud volley of barks, and leapt round us wagging its whole body, wild with glee at finding so many human beings together. It was a large woolly dog, half Airedale, half pariah. For a moment it pranced round us, and then, before anyone could stop it, it had made a dash for the prisoner; and jumping up tried to lick his face. Everyone stood aghast, too taken aback even to grab at the dog.

7   "Who let that bloody brute in here?" said the superintendent angrily. "Catch it, someone!"

8   A warder, detached from the escort, charged clumsily after the dog, but it danced and gambolled just out of his reach, taking everything as part of the game. A young Eurasian jailer picked up a handful of gravel and tried to stone the dog away, but it dodged the stones and came after us again. Its yaps echoed from the jail walls. The prisoner, in the grasp of the two warders, looked on incuriously, as though this was another formality of the hanging. Then we put my handkerchief through its collar and moved off once more, with the dog still straining and whimpering.

9   It was about forty yards to the gallows. I watched the bare brown back of the prisoner marching in front of me. He walked clumsily with his bound arms, but quite steadily, with that bobbing gait of the Indian who never straightens his knees. At each step his muscles slid neatly into place, the lock of hair on his scalp danced up and down, his feet printed themselves on the wet gravel. And once, in spite of the men who gripped him by each shoulder, he stepped slightly aside to avoid a puddle on the path.

10 It is curious, but till that moment I had never realised what it means to destroy a healthy, conscious man. When I saw the prisoner step aside to avoid the puddle, I saw the mystery, the unspeakable wrongness, of cutting a life short when it is in full tide. This man was not dying, he was alive just as we were alive. All the organs of his body were working — bowels digesting food, skin renewing itself, nails growing, tissues forming — all toiling away in solemn foolery. His nails would still be growing when he stood on the drop, when he was falling through the air with a tenth of a second to live. His eyes saw the yellow gravel and the grey walls, and his brain still remembered, foresaw, reasoned — reasoned even about puddles. He and we were a party of men walking together, seeing, hearing, feeling, understanding the same world; and in two minutes, with a sudden snap, one of us would be gone — one mind less, one world less.

11   The gallows stood in a small yard, separate from the main grounds of the prison, and overgrown with tall prickly weeds. It was a brick erection like three sides of a shed, with planking on top, and above that two beams and a crossbar with the rope dangling. The hangman, a grey-haired convict in the white uniform of the prison, was waiting beside his machine. He greeted us with servile crouch as we entered. At a word from Francis the two warders, gripping the prisoner more closely than ever, half led, half pushed him to the gallows and helped him clumsily up the ladder. Then the hangman climbed up and fixed the rope round the prisoner's neck.

12   We stood waiting, five yards away. The warders had formed in a rough circle round the gallows. And then, when the noose was fixed, the prisoner began crying out on his god. It was a high, reiterated cry of "Ram! Ram! Ram! Ram!", not urgent and fearful like a prayer or a cry for help, but steady, rhythmical, almost like the tolling of a bell. The dog answered the sound with a whine. The hangman, still standing on the gallows, produced a small cotton bag like a flour bag and drew it down over the prisoner's face. But the sound, muffled by the cloth, still persisted over and over again: "Ram! Ram! Ram! Ram!"

13   The hangman climbed down and stood ready, holding the lever. Minutes seemed to pass. The steady, muffled crying from the prisoner went on and on, "Ram! Ram! Ram!" never faltering for an instant. The superintendent, his head on his chest, was slowly poking the ground with his stick; perhaps he was counting the cries, allowing the prisoner a fixed number — fifty, perhaps, or a hundred. Everyone had changed colour. The Indians had gone grey like bad coffee, and one or two of the bayonets were wavering. We looked at the lashed, hooded man on the drop, and listened to his cries — each cry another second of life; the same thought was in all our minds: oh, kill him quickly, get it over; stop that abominable noise!

14   Suddenly the superintendent made up his mind. Throwing up his head he made a swift motion with his stick. "Chalo!" he shouted almost fiercely.

15   There was a clanking noise, and then dead silence. The prisoner had vanished, and the rope was twisting on itself. I let go of the dog, and it galloped immediately to the back of the gallows; but when it got there it stopped short, barked, and then retreated into a corner of the yard, where it stood among the weeds, looking timorously out at us. We went round the gallows to inspect the prisoner's body. He was dangling with his toes pointed straight downwards, very slowly revolving, as dead as a stone.

16   The superintendent reached out with his stick and poked the bare body; it oscillated, slightly, "He's all right", said the superintendent. He backed out from under the gallows, and blew out a deep breath. The moody look had gone out of his face quite suddenly. He glanced at his wrist-watch. "Eight minutes past eight. Well, that's all for this morning, thank God".

17   The warders unfixed bayonets and marched away. The dog, sobered and conscious of having misbehaved itself, slipped after them. We walked out of the gallows yard, past the condemned cells with their waiting prisoners, into the big central yard of the prison. The convicts, under the command of warders armed with lathis, were already receiving their breakfast. They squatted in long rows,

each man holding a tin pannikin, while two warders with buckets marched round ladling out rice; it seemed quite a homely, jolly scene, after the hanging. An enormous relief had come upon us now that the job was done. One felt an impulse to sing, to break into a run, to snigger. All at once everyone began chattering gaily.

18   The Eurasian boy walking beside me nodded towards the way we had come, with a knowing smile: "Do you know, sir, our friend (he meant the dead man), when he heard his appeal had been dismissed, he pissed on the floor of his cell. From fright. — Kindly take one of my cigarettes, sir. Do you not admire my new silver case, sir? From the boxwallah, two rupees eight annas. Classy European style."

19   Several people laughed — at what, nobody seemed certain.

20   Francis was walking by the superintendent, talking garrulously: "Well, sir, all hass passed off with the utmost satisfactoriness. It wass all finished — flick! like that. It iss not always so — oah, no! I have known cases where the doctor wass obliged to go beneath the gallows and pull the prisoner's legs to ensure decease. Most disagreeable!"

21   "Wriggling about, eh? That's bad," said the superintendent.

22   "Ach, sir, it iss worse when they become refractory! One man, I recall, clung to the bars of hiss cage when we went to take him out. You will scarcely credit, sir, that it took six warders to dislodge him, three pulling at each leg. We reasoned with him. 'My dear fellow,' we said, 'think of all the pain and trouble you are causing to us!' But no, he would not listen! Ach, he wass very troublesome!"

23   I found that I was laughing quite loudly. Everyone was laughing. Even the superintendent grinned in a tolerant way. "You'd better all come out and have a drink," he said quite genially. "I've got a bottle of whisky in the car. We could do with it."

24   We went through the big double gates of the prison, into the road. "Pulling at his legs!" exclaimed a Burmese magistrate suddenly, and burst into a loud chuckling. We all began laughing again. At that moment Francis's anecdote seemed extraordinarily funny. We all had a drink together, native and European alike, quite amicably. The dead man was a hundred yards away.

(Copyright © George Orwell 1931)

We'll begin with the narrative structure of *A Hanging*. The narrative structure is the way in which any story is related or told.

First of all, some background terminology for you. Literature is made up of three genres, a French word meaning categories, namely: *Drama, Prose* and *Poetry*. So, when anyone decides to commit a story to paper, the first decision that he / she has to take is which of the three genres to employ. That is a decision about structure: the budding writer has to think about the nature of what it is that he / she wants to say and then has to choose which of the three genres is the most appropriate. When I planned this book on textual analysis, I chose the genre of prose: to have written it entirely in verse would have been as pretentious as it would have been inappropriate.

The word "narrative" is an important technical term, applying to all three genres. A narrative is the recounting or relating of a sequence of events, no matter whether that sequence is in poetic, dramatic, or prose form. Indeed the form can be visual — films have a narrative line as indeed do television programmes. Watch the news tonight on television, and you will see that each of the items is told in narrative, the sequence of events usually recounted in chronological order — the order in which they occurred in time.

Within each of the three genres, there are sub-genres. Since Orwell's *A Hanging* is prose, we'll begin with that genre. In prose, there is the distinction between prose fiction and prose non-fiction, though I often feel that this distinction is not as clear-cut as some people try to make out. *A Hanging* is always regarded as *prose non-fiction* because it is written as though it were an eye-witness account of an execution attended by Orwell when he served in Burma. I argue, though, that if you look closely at the structure of the piece you will see a bit of writing that has been so carefully crafted that it's difficult to believe that it is entirely free of imaginative input.

The structure of *A Hanging* seems on the surface to be very simple — and, indeed, that is part of the success of the piece: it has been very straightforwardly put together. It begins outside the prisoner's cell — paragraph 2 — and follows his escorted walk to the gallows. Throughout the piece, the gallows is the focus of attention in the narrative. The distance that the group has to walk is carefully measured for the reader:

> paragraph   6 begins, "We set out for the gallows."
> paragraph   9 begins, "It was about forty yards to the gallows."
> paragraph 11 begins, "The gallows stood in a small yard, . . ."
> paragraph 12 begins, "We stood waiting, five yards away."
> paragraph 13 begins, "The hangman climbed down and stood ready . . ."

As the narrative progresses, the decreasing distance to the gallows creates an increasing concentration on the prisoner himself and on Orwell's reaction to the situation.

But what is really quite fascinating, structurally speaking, is Orwell's use of the incident with the dog. The dog is first introduced as early as paragraph 6:

> Suddenly, when we had gone ten yards, the procession stopped short without any order or warning. A dreadful thing had happened — a dog, come goodness knows whence, had appeared in the yard.

The incident is seen as a "dreadful thing"; the dog had just "appeared" — no explanation is given about where it could have come from or whose dog it might be.

Then comes the touch of irony:

> It came bounding among us wagging its whole body, wild with glee at finding so
> many human beings together.

The dog, in its doggy way, is pleased to see this group because, in its experience, human beings represent fun. The irony is of course that this group of human beings is not going to have fun but is about to engage in the ritualistic killing of one of its members.

The irony is then further intensified by Orwell:

> For a moment it pranced round us, and then, before anyone could stop
> it, it had made a dash for the prisoner; and jumping up tried to lick his
> face. Everyone stood aghast . . .

The implication of their reaction is clear: they are embarrassed and shocked that the dog should select the prisoner as the centre of its fun when they knew — what the dog couldn't know — that it was the prisoner, the very centre of the dog's attention, whose life they were about to end. The superintendent is angry and instructs someone to catch it but the dog continues to highlight the awkwardness — and irony — of the situation by "taking everything as part of the game". The prisoner's reaction is interesting:

> The prisoner, in the grasp of the two warders, looked on incuriously, as though
> this was another formality of the hanging.

The figure at the centre-stage is the one least affected. It is also interesting that it is Orwell's handkerchief that is used to tether the unwitting dog.

Of course this episode with the dog may be true, but it is tempting to think that it has been used deliberately by Orwell as a device — an ironic device — to point up, etch out, highlight the horror in what was happening: the reader inevitably compares and contrasts the dog's reactions with those of the human beings.

What seems more deliberate is how he uses the dog later on in the story as a further measure of the horror: even such a fun-loving, naive, dumb animal as a dog is shocked and finally tamed when it realises that the prisoner is dead:

> I let go of the dog, and it galloped immediately to the back of the gallows; but
> when it got there it stopped short, barked, and then retreated into a corner of the
> yard, where it stood among the weeds, looking timorously out at us.

The dog is used to represent more tellingly than anyone else present those feelings of abused decency that we normally associate with the supposedly more culturally advanced and morally superior nature of human beings.

Another but quite different structural effect of this dog episode is that is serves to delay the narrative, hold it up a fraction, but I shall comment on this more fully later.

The dog episode is also my evidence for suggesting that this piece is not purely non-fiction: Orwell so skilfully crafts the incident with the dog that I cannot help but feel that he is employing dramatic licence. There may have been a dog, but it is used so tellingly that I am certain that it is inspired by Orwell's imagination to enhance the narrative and to establish irony.

Another structural device used by the author is the incident about the puddle; it begins with a description of the prisoner's back in what seems like an interruption to the narrative (paragraph 9):

> . . . I watched the bare brown back of the prisoner marching in front of me. He walked clumsily with his bound arms, but quite steadily, with that bobbing gait of the Indian who never straightens his knees. At each step his muscles slid neatly into place, the lock of hair on his scalp danced up and down, his feet printed themselves on the wet gravel. And once, in spite of the men who gripped him by each shoulder, he stepped slightly aside to avoid a puddle on the path.

There is an emphasis here on normality that adds to the horror: this man is about to be executed, his life deliberately ended, and yet, in spite of the fact that he is about to die in a few minutes' time, his back muscles operate as normal, and he takes the kind of precautions that any normal person would when it comes to puddles.

Everything is outwardly normal and yet we know that the situation is entirely abnormal. This abnormality is heightened by Orwell's contrasting it with the everyday and the commonplace: the muscles sliding into place and the sidestep of the puddle seem so ordinary and, therefore, so dramatically out of place with the hanging.

Orwell then goes on to use these physical observations to make a moral point:

> It is curious, but till that moment I had never realised what it means to destroy a healthy, conscious man. When I saw the prisoner step aside to avoid the puddle, I saw the mystery, the unspeakable wrongness, of cutting a life short when it is in full tide. This man was not dying, he was alive just as we were alive. All the organs of his body were working — bowels digesting food, skin renewing itself, nails growing, tissues forming — all toiling away in solemn foolery. His nails would still be growing when he stood on the drop, when he was falling

through the air with a tenth of a second to live. His eyes saw the yellow gravel and the grey walls, and his brain still remembered, foresaw, reasoned — reasoned even about puddles. He and we were a party of men walking together, seeing, hearing, feeling, understanding the same world; and in two minutes, with a sudden snap, one of us would be gone — one mind less, one world less.

The assumption that we all make — have to make — is that we are going to go on living. The prisoner makes this assumption — cannot help but make it — so he avoids a puddle. His nails go on growing and his skin renews itself. This notion of life going on is emphasised by the use of *walking*, *seeing*, *hearing*, *feeling*, *understanding*: all present particles that stress the continuous nature of action.

This continuity and our assumption of it highlights the horror of the fact that, for one of them, the continuity is about to come to an end — knowingly and deliberately: "in two minutes, with a sudden snap, one of us would be gone". The parallel structure of "one mind less, one world less" effectively stresses the conclusive nature of death. If we are not here to perceive the existence of the world, then, to all intents and purposes, the world no longer exists. We'll also talk about parallel structure at a later point.

Ironically, it is at the edge of death that Orwell makes clear for the reader what it is to be alive, and he does this by selecting and focusing on the kind of ordinary, everyday act that we would normally never notice. That, for me, is what makes him a great writer.

The point made in this central paragraph applies, of course, not only to capital punishment but also to any act of killing: "the unspeakable wrongness (which he goes on to speak about!) of cutting a life short when it is in full tide".

This moral point is not part of the narrative. As we noted earlier, the narrative follows a straightforward structure of concentrating on the man's journey to the gallows. The sequence of events, then, is in chronological order: the events are presented as they happened in time. But this section, where Orwell comments on killing, is not part of that sequence: it is an insertion that is reflective rather than narrative. But it is something else as well: it is in keeping with the increasing *personal* feeling in the passage. The passage begins quite objectively and factually with the group waiting outside the condemned cells; it ends on a highly personal note. At this point — the episode with the puddle — Orwell begins to intensify his personal reaction.

One very interesting aspect of the structure of the piece, which I touched on above and promised I'd return to later, is Orwell's use of delaying tactics, which is part of the author's use of *climax*. The episode of the dog interrupts the narrative and thereby delays the actual moment of the hanging itself. A further delay also takes place just before the execution when the prisoner is allowed time — and quite a lot of time — to pray to his god.

These two delays in the otherwise tight chronological structure increase the reader's suspense and thereby add to the tension of the hanging.

Another aspect of the structure which I find quite fascinating is the extent to which the story continues after the moment of the hanging itself. The hanging takes place in paragraph 15, yet the story doesn't end until paragraph 24. As with the dog and the prisoner's chant, the anecdotes are unexpected and almost out of place.

The anecdotes, however, as always with Orwell, are highly ironic, particularly the story related by Francis about the troublesome prisoner whose struggles to avoid being hanged made life so difficult for the warders. I like particularly: "'We *reasoned* with him.'" Given the situation, the use of the word "reason" seems entirely inappropriate and therefore slightly humorous. This humour helps reduce the considerable tension built up before the execution.

There is something else as well: by its very nature, this prolonged ending further draws attention to the continuity of life. Life for this group of men, clearly, went on after the hanging. And presumably, now that it was over, the rest of the prisoners could get their breakfasts — life goes on.

One final comment on structure before we end this chapter: look how Orwell uses the concept of time. His use of time is significant, given what I have said about his concentration on the continuity of life juxtaposed (placed side by side) with the suddenness of the prisoner's death. Read the passage again and, by yourself, go through it underlining each reference to time. You'll be surprised at how many there are. Once you've done that, then try to work out the contribution that each reference makes to the overall effect of the passage.

You'll be surprised at how easy these tasks are.

CHAPTER FIVE

Situation

A vitally important aspect of an extract that you may well be asked about is *situation*: what is the situation, or setting, of the passage or poem? And remember that setting is not only about place but also about time.

First of all, read carefully the following extract from *The Only Child* by James Kirkup:

> But I seem to recall best a journey we made by tram one winter night. We were going to visit my granny at Westoe, and I was very excited, because an evening excursion was something quite unheard of for me. It had been raining; the gas lamps lit the gleaming pavements and cobbles with a double radiance. The shaking tram wires were sending down showers of white raindrops. Everything in the tram seemed fresh and glittering.

The situation is clearly a journey by tram on a winter's night, but the very fact that the journey is by tram gives a clue that the piece is set some fifty years or more in the past. But, you may argue, there are trams in Amsterdam, Blackpool, even Manchester; what is to say that it isn't set today in one of these cities? If you look closely, however, I think you will detect clues that make clear that the setting isn't modern. Can you find them?

Now read another excerpt from a different book:

> He climbed the crest of the sandhill and gazed about him. Evening had fallen. A rim of the young moon cleft the pale waste of skyline, the rim of a silver hoop embedded in grey sand; and the tide was flowing in fast to the land with a low whisper of her waves, islanding a few last figures in distant pools.

Here it is a bit more difficult to identify the situation. Obviously, it is set by the seaside in the evening, but there is insufficient context to tell us what time of year or even in which year it is set. We come back, time and time again, to this word *context*: situation is very much a product of context, though obviously, in its own way, the situation contributes to that context.

Sometimes you need some biographical information about the author. If I tell you that this extract is from *A Portrait of the Artist as a Young Man* by James Joyce, then you may be better able to say at least in which year, roughly, the passage is set. If you don't know, find out.

I want you to look at a number of extracts and identify the situation (both place and time). Remember all that you have learned: work out as best you can the context and examine carefully the connotations of the words —

Extract A

The church and yew
And farmhouse slept in a Sunday silentness.
The air raised not a straw. The steep farm roof,
With times duskily glowing, entertained
The mid-day sun; and up and down the roof
    White pigeons nestled.
                    Edward Thomas

Extract B

Kino deftly slipped his knife into the edge of the shell. Through the knife he could feel the muscle tighten hard. He worked the blade lever-wise and the closing muscle parted and the shell fell apart. The lip-like flesh writhed up and then subsided. Kino lifted the flesh, and there it lay, the great pearl, perfect as the moon. It captured the light and refined it and gave it back in silver incandescence. It was as large as a seagull's egg. It was the greatest pearl in the world.

                    John Steinbeck

Extract C

. . . the warm heavy smell of turkey and ham and celery rose from the plates and dishes and the great fire was banked high and red in the grate and the green ivy and red holly made you feel so happy and when dinner was ended the big plum pudding would be carried in, studded with peeled almonds and sprigs of holly, with bluish flame running around it and a little green flag flying from the top.

                    James Kirkup

Extract D

The winter evening settles down
With smell of steaks in passageways.
Six o'clock.
The burnt-out ends of smoky days.
And now a gusty shower wraps
The grimy scraps
Of withered leaves about your feet
And newspapers from vacant lots;
The showers beat
On broken blinds and chimney-pots,
And at the corner of the street
A lonely cab-horse steams and stamps.
And then the lighting of the lamps.

                    T.S. Eliot

I realise that I have included a couple of poems among the previous extracts, but don't worry, the methods that I have taught you apply equally to poetry. The textual analysis of poetry at this stage isn't really all that different from the textual analysis of prose.

I hope that you have managed to work out situation, but to help you I shall go through each extract so that you can check your conclusions.

In *Extract A*, the setting is obviously rural — *church and yew and farmhouse* make that very clear. It is mid-day and it is hot — *slept in a Sunday silentness* suggests the languor and lassitude of mid-day heat, as does *the air raised not a straw*. It is also interesting to note, though I do not want you to worry about this just now, that mood is related to the situation — languor, lassitude, silence, warm pleasantness all stem from the mid-day heat. That mood is then intensified by *White pigeons nestled*. Note the author's choice of *nestled* rather than, say, *roosted* or *slept*. *Nestled* clearly contains the word *nest*, not only appropriate, since he is talking about birds, but the word also suggests cosiness, comfort, settling down, and, of course, the pigeons' young. As I say, don't worry because we will deal with mood in the next chapter. Suffice it to say that mood and situation are often very closely linked. What do you think *church* and *yew* suggest?

In *Extract B*, taken from *The Pearl* by John Steinbeck, the situation is quite different. Here we have a pearl fisher who has found an enormous and extremely valuable pearl. Here the situation is easy to identify: mood, in this case, is more difficult to identify, simply because the writer concentrates on a description of the pearl rather than the fisherman's reaction to finding it.

Is, however, finding the pearl an exciting experience? Pleasant? Look at the words that the author uses: "the great pearl", "perfect as the moon", "It captured the light and refined it and gave it back in silver incandescence", "it was as large as a seagull's egg", "It was the greatest pearl in the world". Though these are the author's words — Kino does not speak them — nevertheless, they imply that Kino was delighted with his find and thus convey the mood.

In *Extract C*, identifying the time and place ought not to have been too difficult: "smell of turkey" along with "great fire was banked high and red in the grate" and "red holly" should have suggested Christmas at home to you. Sometimes, quite often really, the words that suggest time and place also suggest mood. Again, situation and mood are interlinked: in this case, the words suggesting Christmas also suggest the mood. Look at: "the big plum pudding . . . studded with peeled almonds and sprigs of holly, with bluish flame", given the context of the entire extract, suggest a mood of congenial domesticity, a homely and happy scene reminiscent of happy childhood. Is there anything else in the extract that confirms my claim about its being about childhood?

Extract D is obviously another poem, but, again, don't be put off by that. You use the same techniques of analysis that we use with prose. In this case, however, it is probably easier to identify mood than situation! Nevertheless, it is clearly winter and night time — "the winter evening". The poet is outside in the street — ". . . a gusty shower wraps / The grimy scraps / Of withered leaves about your feet". Newspapers "from vacant lots" may help define things a little more: do we use, about waste ground, the word "lot" in this country? A clue as to what I mean: the term "parking lot" is American, therefore it is safe to assume that the term "vacant lot" is also American English. Moreover, the words "cab-horse" and "lighting of the lamps" tell us the setting is early twentieth century.

As I said, it is easy to identify mood in this extract. "The burnt out ends of smoky days" suggests the dismalness, the weariness, the languor of wasted days; "grimy scraps" suggests squalor and futility; "withered leaves" suggests decay, which "broken blinds" intensifies.

Situation — and mood — are important aspects of any extract, poem, short story, novel, play, film and are always established right at the beginning, though they can be intensified, developed, or changed as the piece progresses. In textual analysis, you can be fairly certain that you will be asked about both.

Before we end this important chapter, let's look at the very beginning of *Macbeth* by William Shakespeare:

ACT I

Scene I.   *A desert place.*

Thunder and lightning. Enter three Witches.

First Witch:	When shall we three meet again
	In thunder, lightning, or in rain?
Second Witch:	When the hurlyburly's done,
	When the battle's lost and won.
Third Witch:	That will be ere the set of sun.
First Witch:	Where the place?
Second Witch:	Upon the heath.
Third Witch:	There to meet with Macbeth.
First Witch:	I come, Graymalkin!
Second Witch:	Paddock calls.
Third Witch:	Anon.
All:	Fair is foul, and foul is fair:
	Hover through the fog and filthy air. *[Exeunt.]*

You are told that the scene is a desert place, but the fact that it is no more than a "desert" in itself suggests isolation and anonymity. That there is "thunder and lightning" adds a frightening, mysterious, and supernatural aspect to this isolation. The supernatural quality is, of course, confirmed and heightened by the entrance of the three witches. Before a word is spoken, then, we have the situation and mood firmly established.

The first words spoken are: "When shall we three meet again / In thunder, lightning, or in rain?" The thunder and lightning, that is, the elements of the supernatural, are to continue into their next meeting; they themselves are the symbols of the supernatural. Mystery and unearthliness are established. Furthermore, the witches are to meet "When the hurlyburly's done / When the battle's lost and won." What is the "hurly-burly" and how do you reconcile a battle's being both "lost" and "won"? Ambiguity and riddle are added to the charged atmosphere. "Set of sun", "heath", "Graymalkin" "paddock", "fair is foul and foul is fair" are all ingredients of isolation, desolation, witchcraft, and the supernatural. Note the alliteration in "fair is foul and foul is fair", the sound that is produced, as well as the oxymoron and the ambiguity.

Sound? Alliteration? Oxymoron? Ambiguity? I can hear you wondering . . . Read on!

But first of all, let us examine mood in more detail.

CHAPTER SIX

Mood and Word Choice

Words, vocabulary items, as I have said before, have at least two levels of meaning: the denotative and the connotative. Denotative meaning is to do with the *literal* meaning of a word, while connotative meaning is the association that the word has, the mental picture that the word conjures in your mind. The word "picture" suggests that this mental image is visual, but of course the image can be associated with smell, taste, hearing, or touch as well as sight.

Authors are very much aware of the connotations of words and deliberately choose those words, the connotations of which suit their purpose. Again, let's look at the beginning of *A Hanging*.

> It was in Burma, a sodden morning of the rains. A sickly light, like yellow tinfoil, was slanting over the high walls into the jail yard. We were waiting outside the condemned cells, a row of sheds fronted with double bars, like small animal cages. Each cell measured about ten feet by ten and was quite bare within except for a plank bed and a pot of drinking water. In some of them brown silent men were squatting at the inner bars, with their blankets draped round them. These were the condemned men, due to be hanged within the next week or two.

The first sentence makes clear the setting: Burma and it is the rainy season. But again, look how the setting contributes to the mood. You cannot help but notice words such as *sodden, rains, sickly light, yellow tinfoil, slanting*. What do these words suggest to you? What kind of atmosphere — or mood — do they conjure up? Is that mood in keeping with the story that unfolds? The word *sickly* suggests not only the notion of decay but also the idea of things being ill or wrong. What do you think that *yellow tinfoil* suggests? Think about colour and texture.

While the denotative meanings of *high walls* and *jail yard* are vital to the narrative — we have to know that this is set in a high security jail — yet for all of us the words *jail* combined with *high walls* have connotations of unpleasantness and restriction. Again, these words, along with the other words quoted above, contribute to the overall mood of the passage: one of sadness, decay, unpleasantness, foreboding, and constraint.

Moreover, rain is often used by writers (and film directors) as a symbol of sadness. Rain and storms can reinforce the notion of foreboding, disaster, imminent tragedy. Shakespeare often exploits rain and storms when he wants to create the feeling that something terrible is about to happen — you need only think of *King Lear*. Rain, as you can read from the opening of *A Hanging*, is very carefully and cleverly used by Orwell to suggest a tragic mood. How does the word *sodden* reinforce the ideas suggested by rain?

Mood, then, is created by word choice, and when you are asked to comment on the mood of an extract look at the words chosen by the author, think of the connotations of these words within the context that you find them, and show how the connotations contribute to the atmosphere.

Let's take a break from *A Hanging* and examine another piece altogether. We have already looked at an extract from *The Only Child* by James Kirkup; let's now look at a bit more of it. We have already talked briefly about the mood but this time we'll examine mood a little more thoroughly. We will look at the word choice to see how the words chosen by the author contribute to the mood that we have already identified.

> But I seem to recall best a journey we made by tram one winter night. We were going to visit my granny at Westoe, and I was very excited, because an evening excursion was something quite unheard of for me. It had been raining; the gas lamps lit the gleaming pavements and cobbles with a double radiance. The shaking tram wires were sending down showers of white raindrops. Everything in the tram seemed fresh and glittering. The breezy windows sparkled with long zigzags of rain and the passing street lamps gorgeously flared through the panels of blue and yellow and ruby glass. Outside, it was cold and windy, and we could feel the gale buffeting against the side of the tram, making it sway and lurch more than usual, and throwing the passengers against one another. There were bursts of laughter and snatches of song, and the fresh, clean, cold sea-wind was blowing right through the upper deck. Above, a high half-moon seemed to be skidding along on its back through piles of black white-lined rags. It was a wild night, with a sense of magic in the offing. The people in the tram did not seem like ordinary mortals; a kind of exhilarating gaiety had seized them, and it seemed to lighten their bodies and illuminate their faces. At times I was sure we were really flying.
>
> *James Kirkup*

This passage is set in rain and gales, but is the mood tragic? We need to look at the author's word choice within the overall context.

The context is a tram journey undertaken on a rough winter's night, but words such as *excited, excursion, gleaming pavements, double radiance, showers of white raindrops, fresh and glittering, breezy windows, sparkled, gorgeously flared* give an altogether pleasing, happy picture, one of adventure in a spectacularly attractive world. The scene, far from being depressing or foreboding, reveals the beauty of a winter's night.

When you are asked about word choice, however, it is not enough merely to quote the words; you have to comment on how they contribute to the mood or atmosphere or image that you have identified. How does, for example, *excited* contribute to the idea of an enjoyable excursion in mid-winter? The idea that the author is recalling the journey and that he was thrilled by something so simple as a tram journey creates, for me anyway, the idea that he is a little boy: *excited* contributes to this notion because it conveys the feelings of simple wonderment and enjoyment that little boys have on journeys such as the one being described.

That the pavements were *gleaming* conveys an attractiveness that pavements don't always have, especially in mid-winter, and *double radiance* develops and reinforces that attractiveness, as though the light refracted by the rain is almost like the light from fireworks. This notion is continued in *the shaking tram wires were sending down showers of white raindrops*. Since all of you are too young to remember trams, this isn't just a reference to weather but could also refer to the flash of sparks created by the tram's pantograph breaking contact with the electric wire overhead. You can see how the image is one of dazzling brilliance.

Now you try it for yourself. Examine the other words that I selected — *fresh and glittering*, *breezy windows*, *sparkled*, *gorgeously flared* — and comment on each one, showing in turn how the word or phrase contributes to the overall picture that we have identified. It's easy, isn't it?

The next task that you must attempt for yourself is to go through the rest of the passage, identify similar words, and then comment on each one, making clear its contribution to the overall picture.

If you are asked about word choice — and in textual analysis, questions about word choice are inevitable — follow these simple steps:

1. *What is your overall impression of the passage — is it sad, happy, foreboding, tragic, humorous? Go by your personal response.*

2. *Identify the words that help contribute to that reaction.*

3. *Comment on how each of the words makes that contribution.*

Sometimes writers make up words or change words to suit their purpose. Ted Hughes in *Pike*, for example, talks about the pike being *jungled* in weed, where clearly he has taken the noun *jungle* and creates a new verb. Inventing words can bring a liveliness and vigour to writing, if used sparingly and accurately.

Remember this extract?

> He climbed the crest of the sandhill and gazed about him. Evening had fallen. A rim of the young moon cleft the pale waste of skyline, the rim of a silver hoop embedded in grey sand; and the tide was flowing in fast to the land with a low whisper of her waves, islanding a few last figures in distant pools.

I think you'll agree that this is a highly atmospheric piece, capturing with tight precision the falling of dusk by the seashore. But note the word *islanding*: the author has taken the noun *island* and created a new verb, and he has used the present participle form (the bit of the verb that ends in *ing*) to suggest movement that is continuous. He captures and emphasises the speed of the tide: it is flowing so fast that it is creating islands of sand. There is also the notion of *isolating* the figures on these islands.

If this all seems a bit much, don't worry — we'll keep talking about word choice again and again.

CHAPTER SEVEN

Literary Devices

Sound and Alliteration

Let's begin this chapter by examining sound — the sounds that we make when we speak. There are, as you know, five vowels in English: *a*, *e*, *i*, *o*, and *u*. We can pronounce these vowels as in *hate*, *feed*, *pine*, *slope*, and *cute*. The sound produced by pronouncing these vowels this way is known as *long vowel sound*. We can, however, pronounce these vowels with a *short vowel sound* as in *hat*, *fed*, *pin*, *slop*, and *cut*. What is important to note is that the long vowel sounds tend to be more pleasant than the short vowel sounds.

But there is more to it than that. The other letters are known as consonants and can be grouped into types of sounds as follows:

Letter	Type of Sound	Sound Effect
b and p	Plosive	hard
hard c, g, qu, and k	Guttural	harsh, often unpleasant
d and t	Dental	neutral
f , th, and v	Fricative	can be unpleasant when combined with a short vowel
l, w, and y	Liquid	mellifluous and pleasant, but the *w* sound can be mean
m and n	Nasal	usually pleasant
soft c, s, and z	Sibilant	soporific or hissing
r	Rolling	almost like a vowel

It is the combination of the consonant and the vowel sound that creates the effect. For example, it is no accident that our most effective and unpleasant swearing words begin with the plosive *b* followed by a short vowel sound. Good taste prevents me from giving you an example! If you are about to hammer a nail home, and, instead of hitting the nail, you hit your thumb, I am willing to wager that you will automatically form the *b* sound with your lips, as in "Oh, ya b......!"

I have always thought that the nastiest of the four letter words isn't a swearing word at all, but is the word *work* pronounced with a strong Scottish accent: the *w* is tightly formed by drawing the lips together to form the meanest shape you can imagine and then the vowel is pronounced with a harsh guttural *u* — *"Ye need to wurk, laddie, and wurk hard!"*

Let's look at some more extracts:

Extract A

> What could they offer us for bait?
> Our captain was brave and we were true . . .
> There was a little private gate,
> A little wicked wicket gate.
> A wizened warder let them through.
>
> *Edwin Muir*

Extract B

> Bent double, like old beggars under sacks,
> Knock-kneed, coughing like hags, we cursed through sludge,
> Till on the haunting flares we turned our backs,
> And towards our distant rest began to trudge.
>
> *Wilfred Owen*

Extract C

> O for a draught of vintage! That hath been
>   Cool'd a long age in the deep-delved earth,
> Tasting of Flora and the country green,
>   Dance, and Provençal song, and sunburnt mirth!
> O for a beaker full of the warm South,
>   Full of the true, the blushful Hippocrene,
>   With beaded bubbles winking at the brim,
>   And purple-stained mouth;
> That I might drink, and leave the world unseen,
>   And with thee fade away into the forest dim:
>
> *John Keats*

Extract D

>   Flowered curtains, thin and frayed,
> Fall to within five inches of the sill.
>
> *Philip Larkin*

I hope that you've been noticing for yourself the sound effects of the letters as you read the extracts. Look again at Extract A: the vowel sounds in the first two lines are mostly long — "bait", the second syllable of "captain", "brave" and "true". These long comforting sounds support the ideas of bravery and security. Look carefully, though, at the following three lines. The vowel sounds suddenly become short and, combined with the unpleasant consonants, the short, ugly sounds support the ideas of meanness and betrayal: "little wicked wicket gate", "a wizened warder let them through". The *w* is a mean sound. Mean people, it is commonly held, have small drawn-in mouths with the permanent shape of someone forming the letter *w*. Try to form the letter and you'll see what I mean. This mean *w* is then followed by the unpleasant short *i* followed by the guttural *ck*. The word *wicked* almost sounds the same as it means!

In Extract B, the situation is clearly unpleasant in the extreme: First World War soldiers are returning from the front. "Cursed through sludge" and "haunting flares" are clues to the fact that it is World War I. This time the hard *b* sound is used extensively in conjunction with short syllables, as are the gutturals *k*, hard *g*, and *ck* to create a powerful image of the noise of battle. Moreover, the poet exploits the fricative in an unpleasant way: *coughing*, for example, which is almost onomatopoeic, where the sound represents the meaning.

In Extract C, the situation is different again. The mood is a celebration of wine, and the sound supports that celebratory feel. This time the *b* sounds aren't harsh, but accentuate the idea of a cupful of wine bursting to the brim with colour and flavour. There is an earthy (*deep-delved earth*), cool (*cool'd for a long age*), sensuous (*tasting of Flora and country green*) feel to the image, that is vibrant (*Dance, and Provençal song, and sunburnt mirth*) and colourful (*blushful* and *purple-stained*). The richness of all this imagery is well supported by the rich sounds produced by the plosives, the dentals, the sibilants, the fricatives, all combined with the long pleasant vowel sounds.

Getting the idea? The last extract should be very easy for you. It is from *Mr Bleaney* by Philip Larkin. The poet creates in us the impression that Mr Bleaney's room is bare, neglected, and shabby. These two lines contribute to that impression. The tone is, then, one of neglect and shabbiness. Note how the sounds contribute to that tone: the fricatives, combined with the short vowel sounds, are unpleasant and contribute the notion of decay and neglect — the curtains are in poor taste, are too short, and are frayed — the word, again, is almost onomatopoeic.

The important lesson to learn from all this is that it is not enough to be able to spot, say, alliteration; you have also to be able to say in what ways that alliteration is effective. Now you can do that — you can point to the alliteration and show how the situation and / or tone is being supported by that particular combination of consonants and vowel sounds. Sound, then, is closely related to and supports meaning.

CHAPTER EIGHT

Other Literary Devices

Metaphor and Irony

Metaphor

I have devoted a whole chapter to sound because I think that candidates believe that it is a very difficult concept to understand and write about. I hope that you now realise how much easier it is to discuss sound than you thought.

The other literary devices are probably more familiar to you. There are many of them (see page 45, Table A), but I want only to deal with metaphor and irony — partly because of their importance and partly because everything else really relates to them. Lastly, in the next chapter, I shall deal with rhythm and rhyme, which are also connected to sound.

Probably the most important of all the literary devices is *metaphor*. Notice that I don't say *a metaphor* but simply *metaphor*, and that distinction is important. Metaphor has to do with comparisons: it is where you say that one thing is like another (referred to as simile) or, indeed, where one thing *is* another. For example, in the two statements:

> *Kevin was like a lion in the fight*; or
>
> *Kevin was a lion in the fight*

there are two terms — *Kevin* and *lion*. The statements compare Kevin to being like a lion or having lion-like qualities. Let's call *Kevin* term *A* and *lion-like* term *B*. Of the two terms *A* and *B*, the statement is saying that *A* has the qualities of *B*, but the statement does not say that *B* has the qualities of *A* — and that's important. In other words, Kevin has the qualities of a lion, but the metaphor does not say that lions have the qualities that Kevin has: they may well have, but that is beside the point!

Let's put it another way:

As I said, call the subject (in this case Kevin) term *A* and the thing to which the subject is being compared term *B*. Then sct out the sentence as follows —

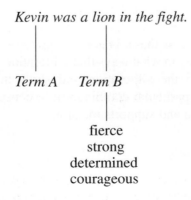

Kevin was a lion in the fight.

Term A   Term B

fierce
strong
determined
courageous

We know, then, that Kevin fought, *fiercely, strongly, determinedly, courageously*.

We can now say whether or not the metaphor is effective. If Kevin did not fight with ferocity, strength, determination, and courage, then the metaphor is *not* appropriate. If, however, that is exactly how Kevin fought, then the metaphor is appropriate, therefore effective.

Let's try another one:

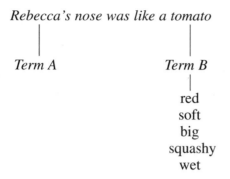

Now ask yourself if the metaphor is appropriate — if it describes Rebecca's nose accurately, then it is appropriate and therefore effective.

When considering Term *B*, think of what the object looks like, smells like, tastes like, sounds like, feels like to the touch. Not all will be appropriate, but each is worth considering.

In other words, think of the FIVE SENSES.

Sometimes, however, the metaphor is not always obvious. Look at this example:

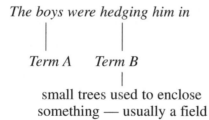

If the boys were actually enclosing him the way in which trees can enclose a small space then the metaphor is appropriate and therefore effective. However, it is not a particularly startling metaphor, and you might want to say that it lacks originality.

Metaphor then compares the *A* term with the *B* term, saying that the *A* term has the qualities of the *B* term or, at least, that the *B* term makes a comment on the *A* term.

In the example:

Sid is a snake in the grass

we know that Sid has the qualities that we associate with snakes: sneakiness, baseness, slyness, duplicity. Maybe you need to look up the word *duplicity* in the dictionary — that's a good habit to develop.

You notice that in each of these statements the reader is presented with an image — a mental picture of lions and tomatoes and snakes. An image is a mental picture, though an image is not always pictorial. Some images have to do with sound, others with taste and smell, others with touch. In other words, images appeal to our five senses, but the image is often metaphorical. The image (the *B* term) comments on the thing to which it is referring (the *A* term).

Advertising exploits the idea of metaphor. Look at almost any advert and you will find that an image is created. The image (term *B*) is there to suggest the qualities possessed by the product (term *A*). Modern British advertising often uses very sophisticated images at a highly metaphorical level to communicate to consumers the qualities of the product being advertised. Sometimes the imagery is so sophisticated and clever that I can remember the image better than I can remember the name of the product being advertised!

In advertising, especially television advertising, the image is more than just a comparison between term *A* and term *B*; the advert is presented as a complete story — a narrative that in itself is metaphorical. The story, by its characters or its setting, suggests the qualities of the product being advertised. Sometimes, and, more simply, the narrative is merely a vehicle to allow the qualities of the product to be stated. We, however, are in the business of textual analysis, and, no matter how interesting advertising may be, it is for others to explore its metaphorical devices. But when next you see or read an advert, be aware of the metaphors that are being exploited.

Metaphor, then, is a device of comparison. But it is also, in a sense, the basis of all literature in that all stories are metaphorical: the story itself makes a comparative comment on the nature of human existence. For example, *Hamlet* is about a young prince who is commanded by his father's ghost to undertake the revenge of his father's murder. In the days in which *Hamlet* is set, revenge was not only expected, it was part of the moral climate of the time. Hamlet, however, an intelligent and sensitive young man, questions the very nature of revenge: he belongs to a different moral order quite out of keeping with the times. His dilemma, his inability to commit what he sees as cold-blooded killing, even of a man he detests, is a dilemma of opposing moral codes — a position with which we can all identify by dint of the fact we are human and human beings can be faced with such dilemmas. The play, then, is a metaphor for the human condition.

This notion of metaphor can be extended to all aspects of literature: of an image itself, of a short poem, of a short story, of a self-contained extract, or of an episode of *Eastenders*. If we understand this, we understand how literature works and that also makes the job of analysing it all the easier.

One of the ways to assess the effectiveness of a metaphor is to analyse its appropriateness — in other words, is term *B* appropriate in its comparison with and comment on term *A*? Let's look at a few examples:

Hamlet: Fie on't, ah, fie, 'tis an unweeded garden That grows to seed. Things rank and gross in nature Possess it merely.

Hamlet has been talking about this world and its uses: here he compares the world to an unweeded garden. How appropriate is this comparison? It certainly gives us a clue about his state of mind if he sees the world as an *unweeded* garden; one that isn't tended or cared for and where ugliness is allowed to prevail.

Look, though, how Shakespeare develops the metaphor. In this unweeded garden, *things rank and gross possess it merely*. You need to know that the word *merely* has changed its meaning in the last 400 years — in Shakespeare's time it meant *entirely*. But what are *rank* things? He is obviously referring to the weeds. Let me give you a clue: we still use *rank* about smells. *Gross* still means repellently fat and ugly. Is the metaphor, then, appropriate and is its development consistent with what Shakespeare is trying to say?

Let's take another example:

> Somewhere in sands of the desert
> A shape with lion body and the head of a man,
> A gaze blank and pitiless as the sun,
> Is moving its slow thighs, while all about it
> Reel shadows of the indignant desert birds.

Clearly, there is no beast that has a shape with lion body and the head of a man; the image created here by W.B. Yeats is metaphorical. From the qualities that he has made clear in the term *B* of the metaphor, what do you imagine are the qualities of term *A* and to what might he be referring? What do you make of the *indignant desert birds* that *reel shadows* about this metaphorical beast?

Obviously, if you have studied Yeats, you will be better able to identify the metaphor, but even if you haven't, you can still say something about the image and its appropriateness.

Metaphor, then, is to do with comparing one thing to another: and it really is vitally important to remember this whether we are considering the effectiveness of a metaphor or the effectiveness of the metaphorical significance of a piece of literature.

Irony

Irony is one of those words that everyone recognises but few can define. You can recognise the irony in a situation, but probably have difficulty in explaining it. Try to remember that irony involves the bringing together of two words or ideas or even objects, which in themselves are unironic but, when brought together, imply a contrast that is significant.

It's often best, when trying to explain as something as complex as irony, to think of an example: a packet of cigarettes is, in itself, unironic, as is a packet of vitamin pills, but when you place the cigarettes side by side with the vitamin pills, the one makes an ironic comment on the other.

Do you remember that in *A Hanging*, we noted the ironic use of the dog? Look at page 20 to remind yourself. Orwell established the irony by describing the dog as "wild with glee at seeing so many human beings together": the dog associates fun with this species, yet these very members of this species are about to do something as unfunny as you can get. The contrast is ironic and all the more heightened because the dog remains innocent — until the very end — of what these people are about to do to one of the group. The irony is then developed further when Orwell has the dog select the prisoner for his special attention — the very member of the group about to be hanged!

There is another kind of irony — sometimes referred to as *dramatic irony*, simply because it occurs in drama. Again, it's best to examine an example. In *Macbeth*, by William Shakespeare, King Duncan is being told by his son, Malcolm, about the way in which the traitor, Cawdor, reacted to his execution. Cawdor, it seems, confessed his previous traitorous acts and died repentantly and bravely. Duncan comments that Cawdor had been:

> *a gentleman on whom I built*
> *An absolute trust.*

As Duncan says these words, the stage direction indicates: *Enter Macbeth* — the very man who will assassinate Duncan.

Do you see the irony?

Again, from the same play, when Duncan arrives at Macbeth's castle, the very place in which he is to be murdered, he says:

> *This castle hath a pleasant seat; the air*
> *Nimbly and sweetly recommends itself*
> *Unto our gentle senses.*

Ironic?

Dramatic irony is when the audience knows the implication of a speech or an action, but where at least one of the characters on stage is unaware of these implications. I think that all irony, even in real life, is heightened when at least one person present doesn't realise that the situation is ironic.

Irony pervades literature — it is used in novels, plays, poems, films and even advertising. Indeed, I often think that if you want to spot the various literary devices and understand how they operate, you could do worse than study a few adverts! There you will find alliteration, use of sound and rhythm, personification, narrative structure, metaphor and irony. Not to mention hyperbole — gross exaggeration!

I have compiled a table of the various literary devices that are used by authors. The list is neither exclusive nor exhaustive, but I trust that it is helpful. Study it and refer to it when you are tackling textual analysis — or even your Specialist Study — or indeed when you are puzzled by some question in the interpretation!

Literary/Poetic Techniques — *for use with Interpretation as well as Textual Analysis and Critical Essay*
Table A

Literary Technique	Explanation	Example	Effect
Alliteration (to do with sound)	Repetition of consonants: b,c,d,f,g,h,j,k,l,m,n,p,q,r,s,t,v,w,x,y,z	*The rifles' rapid rattle*	To draw attention to the words and make them memorable; to ensure a connection between the words; to make the sound of the words support the sense and strengthen the meaning; to contribute to rhythm.
Assonance (to do with sound)	Repetition of the vowel sound: a, e, i, o, u	*You do not do, you do not do / Any more black shoe*	To draw the reader's attention to the words and make them memorable; to make the sound of the words support the sense and strengthen the meaning; to contribute to rhythm; in this case, to capture childish sounds.
Onomatopoeia (to do with sound)	Where the sound of a word echoes the meaning	*Bang! Wallop!*	To draw attention to the words; sometimes to create a comic effect; to make the sound of the words support the sense and strengthen the meaning.
Metaphor	Where one thing is compared to another	*Larry was a lion in the fight*	In a metaphor there are two terms being compared — Term *A* and Term *B*: the qualities of Term *B* are used to describe Term *A*.
Simile	Same as a metaphor, but uses the words "like" or "as"	*Larry was **like** a lion in the fight*	As in metaphor.
Metonymy	A device of representation, where a part of something represents the whole	*I see a sail!*	The word *sail* represents the sailing ship. The logo of a company is used to represent all the qualities of that company

45

Literary Technique	Explanation	Example	Effect
Oxymoron	Juxtaposition (placing side by side) of opposites	*bitter sweet, still splashes, submarine delicacy*	To make the idea memorable; to highlight irony; to support the complexity of the author's meaning.
Irony	The bringing together of two words, ideas, or even objects such that a contrast is implied and each thereby comments on the other	*A packet of vitamin pills placed beside a packet of of cigarettes*	To add a new level of meaning and to support what the author is saying — often to create an amusing effect.
Sarcasm	Where you state the opposite of what you mean in order to ridicule	*Saying "Well done" to a pupil who is struggling to answer a question*	To ridicule the person and to make others laugh.
Parenthesis	Additional information isolated from the rest of a sentence by paired dashes, paired brackets, or paired commas	*I went to the pub — the one on the corner — and had a drink*	Provides the reader with necessary additional information that adds clarity or even definition.
Present Participle	Those bits of the verb that end in -ing	*growing, jumping, running, walking, dancing, working*	Draws attention to the presentness and continuity of the action — the fact that the action is continuing at this moment.
Hyperbole	Gross exaggeration	*All the perfumes of Arabia will ne'er sweeten this little hand*	Again draws attention to and supports meaning.
Transferred Epithet	When a word is transferred from its usual associations to an unusual association	*Fitting the clumsy helmet just in time*	Draws attention to the clumsiness.

Literary Technique	Explanation	Example	Effect
Enjambement	A poetic device where the poet uses run-on lines	*Hatless, I take off* *My cycle clips in awkward* *reverence,* *Move forward, run my hand* *around the font*	Allows the poet to draw attention to words and to create surprise by delaying the word to the next line. Sometimes creates tension especially if there is a run-on verse.
Rhyme Scheme	*a a b b (rhyming couplet):* *a b a b :* *a b a b c d e c d e*	Usually comic effect. Traditional effect — usually serious. Rhyme scheme of *Whitsun Weddings* — complex — captures the complexity of the thought in the poem.	
Para-rhyme (a near rhyme)	Last verse of *Whitsun Weddings*: Larkin rhymes *again* with *rain*	Has a haunting effect, the sound of the word *rain* echoes but doesn't really rhyme with the sound *again*.	
Personification	Where you give inanimate objects the qualities of a live human being.	*Destination board of bus:* *"I'm sorry, I'm not in* *service"*	Effect can vary — in this case it is to give a bus a personality and make it less impersonal since it is not providing a service at the time.
Climax	The build-up to a powerful or dramatic point	*Storms on the hills* *Gather their thunderous* *clouds, overhead* *Mass the monstrous* *battalions of the skies —*	Dramatic effect in the build up to the most important past of the sentence or verse — also contributes to the rhythm.
Anti-climax	The opposite of climax	*Doth sometimes counsel take* *and sometimes tea*	Humour, usually.

Literary Technique	Explanation	Example	Effect
Zeugma — Condensed sentence	Where two words or ideas are linked together often to create an anti-climactic or comic effect	*The last confetti and advice were thrown*	Larkin links concrete idea with an abstract one creating anti-climax.
Anthropomorphism	Attributing human characteristics to animals	*It ticks the second they must climb / into a narrow nest (Of birds)*	Climb is an unusual word to use about birds and the anthropomorphism draws attention to the meaning.

CHAPTER NINE

Other Literary Devices

Rhythm and Rhyme

I suspect that the words *rhythm* and *rhyme* are the two words most likely to drain you of whatever confidence I have succeeded in building up. A question that demands comment on the rhythm and / or rhyme of a piece of text is guaranteed to strike fear into the hearts of many, but, as you will find out, commenting on rhythm and rhyme really isn't that difficult. Both are related to sound. We have already studied sound in an earlier chapter, but I now want to examine its relationship with rhythm and rhyme.

Most people probably associate rhythm / rhyme and sound with poetry, but prose, too, has a rhythm that is often as effective as the rhythm of poetry. We are going to begin with prose. There is a strong connection between sentence structure and rhythm: you are often asked to comment, both in textual analysis and in the interpretation, on sentence structure — and the answer is often that the sentence structure is in the form of a list, but why are lists effective? The answer can often be that they are effective because they create a rhythm which supports meaning. For example, in the following extract, the author, Robert Louis Stevenson, is talking about Edinburgh's climate:

> She is liable to be beaten upon by all the winds that blow, to be drenched with rain, to be buried in cold sea fogs out of the east, and powdered with the snow as it comes flying southwards from the Highland hills.

Let's take a question that you could well be asked: *What effects are achieved by the sentence structure of this sentence?* You need to begin by establishing what that sentence structure is — clearly a list. Why is the list effective? Because it draws attention to the items in it, thereby reinforcing meaning — in this case the author wants to stress the horror of the weather that comes from all directions and the list structure helps to achieve that effect.

But there is something else as well: the list is in parallel structure — that is, the items in it are structured in the same way. In this case, Stevenson repeats the *to be . . . by all the* structure and that creates a rhythm which also helps to reinforce meaning by capturing the sound that the elements make as they bear down on the capital city. Note also the use of alliteration, which contributes to the rhythm. Altogether, the list, the parallel structure, the alliteration, the rhythm combine to make the whole sentence memorable.

The next sentence in this same extract is similar in structure and effect:

> The weather is raw and boisterous in winter, shifty and ungenial in summer, and a downright meteorological purgatory in spring.

Again we note that it is a list, and that the list is in parallel structure: note that each of the paired adjectives — *raw and boisterous* and *shifty and ungenial* — increase in the number of syllables: *raw and boisterous* has five syllables and *shifty and ungenial* has seven and that *downright meteorological purgatory* has 13. In other words, there is a build up of syllables — a build up of sound within the parallel structure that adds considerable *climax* to the sentence. That build up or climax of sound supports the meaning, which is that the weather gets worse as you move to spring, not better!

The point to note, of course, is the contribution of the sound to meaning. Listen carefully to the rhythm of the sentence that you are reading, listen for a build up of sound leading to a climax and try to work out how all of that contributes to the meaning of the sentence. If a writer is talented (and we could be talking about you!) then he or she will be skilled in the use of climax to contribute to and support the meaning of his / her work.

There are other sound devices: you already know about alliteration — the repetition of consonants and the effects that such a sound device can create. But, of course, alliteration and assonance (the repetition of vowel sounds) contribute to rhythm, creating a slow or a fast pace. Read carefully the opening verse of *Timothy Winters* by Charles Causley:

Timothy Winters comes to school	*a*
With eyes as wide as a football-pool,	*a*
Ears like bombs and teeth like splinters:	*b*
A blitz of a boy is Timothy Winters.	*b*

Without doubt, the *a a b b* rhyme scheme helps create the very fast pace — and humorous effect — of this poem. The rhyming of the two syllables of *splinters* with *Winters* adds to the humour (we call the rhyming of more than one syllable *feminine rhyme*), but this rhyme also adds to the fast pace of the poem. More than that, though, look at the effect of the alliteration on the rhythm: the repetition of the hard *b* sound in the last two lines speeds up the lines — and helps draw attention to the connection between the words *bombs*, *blitz* and *boy*.

What matters about rhythm and sound — as with all literary devices — is to use your common sense. Ask yourself *how* the rhythm and sound, created by sentence structure and sound devices, is contributing to the overall effect.

A perfect example of what I am talking about can be found at the end of the Barry Lopez extract in Chapter 1. To save you going back to Chapter 1, I have reproduced the last three sentences for you:

> *Cortés, relentless and vengeful, returned to the Valley of Mexico eleven months later with a larger army and laid siege to the city. Canal by canal, garden by garden, home by home, he destroyed what he had described to Charles V as "the most beautiful city in the world". On June 16, in a move calculated to humiliate and frighten the Mexican people, Cortés set fire to the aviaries.*

This is a really interesting piece of writing, brilliantly executed. Look at the first of these two sentences: immediately following the word "Cortés" the author inserts the phrase "relentless and vengeful" — a phrase which makes clear the mood that Cortés is in and draws attention to the two words "relentless" and "vengeful". In the final two sentences, the author then develops both of these ideas. Look at the sentence structure of the second last (penultimate) sentence: the repetition of the phrase structure (x by x, y by y, z by z) develops the relentlessness by showing how calculatingly and methodically and deliberately Cortés went about the business of destroying the city. Note also that such repetition contributes to the sound and rhythm of the sentence, which in turn draws attention to the meaning — i.e., his relentlessness.

Cortés's vengeful nature is shown by the fact that he destroyed what he had previously described as "the most beautiful city in the world". But perhaps the vengeance is best shown by the structure of the last sentence, which is in the form of climax. The climax — *Cortés set fire to the aviaries* — is achieved by ensuring that it comes at the very end of the piece and by the writer's careful build-up of phrases. The normal sentence order in English suggests that the sentence should read *Cortés set fire to the aviaries on June 16 in a move calculated to humiliate and frighten the Mexican people*, but Lopez, by taking the phrases *on June 16* and *in a move calculated to humiliate and frighten the Mexican people* and by putting them at the beginning of the sentence, creates a build-up thereby delaying the punch-line. Such a technique makes the conclusion to the passage all the more effective and powerful.

You see now the ways in which sentence structure is a vital part of rhythm and how rhythm contributes to meaning and to effect?

Let's read one more piece. It's back to Orwell again, this time from his final sentence of *Why I Write*, a piece of prose in which Orwell makes clear his motives for being a journalist:

> And looking back through my work, I see that it is invariably where I lacked a political purpose that I wrote lifeless books and was betrayed into purple passages, sentences without meaning, decorative adjectives and humbug generally.

You probably need to know that the word *humbug* means hypocrisy. Because this is the final sentence of the essay, you would most likely be asked to examine how effective the sentence is as a conclusion to the piece.

Now I realise that, in all probability, you haven't read the rest of the essay, but that doesn't stop us, for the purposes of this question, from trying to answer it! How effective as a conclusion? The first thing that you would do is look for concluding type words or phrases — and they are there. The phrase *And looking back through my work* suggests conclusion — the idea of looking back through something invariably signals a conclusion. But, now that you know about sentence structure and rhythm and sound, you can give a more developed and sophisticated answer.

The first comment that you would no doubt make is that the sentence is in the form of a list and that the items in that list are climactically structured — there is a build-up from the general — *lifeless books* to the increasingly particular — *purple passages* to the more particular *sentences without meaning* right down to particular words — *decorative adjectives*. Then the writer takes us finally back to the general again with the final item in the list — *humbug generally*.

But also examine the rhythm of the sentence. Not only is there a build-up in the ideas of the items in the list, there is a build-up in the rhythm to the final crescendo of *humbug generally*. There is a delay in getting to the final notion of humbug and that delay is deliberately brought about by the rhythm of the piece. Take out one of the items in the list and you will see what I mean!

Conclusions, then, are effective not just because they draw together the ideas of the passage, often signalled by a concluding word or phrase, but because there is some kind of climactic rhythm that has the effect of suggesting finality. You should remember that in your own writing! Not only that, but it is beside your conclusion that the marker will put his or her mark!

CHAPTER TEN

Evaluation or Appreciation

You will know by now that textual analysis involves *evaluation* or *appreciation*. Such questions really are quite easy, and we have already covered much of what is meant by evaluation.

To recap: I have stressed the importance of the three questions —

(a) *What is the passage / poem / extract about?*

(b) *What effects does the piece have on me?*

(c) *How have these effects been achieved?*

You will have been taught by your teacher that textual analysis, as with interpretation, involves three ideas — Understanding, Analysis and Evaluation. You will also have been taught that personal reaction is an important aspect of textual analysis and other aspects of literary study. But the three questions that we have dealt with will help you enormously.

The answer to question *(a)*, for example, involves the themes or issues raised by the text — i.e., it deals with Understanding. The answer to question *(b)* involves Personal Reaction, though the identification of the effects also involves analysis. The answer to question *(c)* clearly involves analysis and evaluation — having analysed the ways in which the effects have been achieved, you can be asked to evaluate the effects.

How do you do that, you wonder? It really is quite straightforward. Look back at Chapter Eight and you will see that you have already learned to evaluate metaphor — you have learned to say whether or not it is appropriate and therefore effective. That is really what evaluation is about — if you are able to say that a device (any literary device) is effective then you are able to evaluate it.

Let's now take an example of a developed — or extended — metaphor. The extract below, written by Melvyn Bragg in 1983, is taken from an article in which he argues that the BBC's solutions to the problems of increasing competition may stretch the Corporation too far and may ultimately destroy it. He claims that the BBC's plans are —

> like stretching glass more and more elaborately, more and more thinly until the strain becomes unbearable. The heat of the eighties and the flaw in the ambition could bring about the most almighty crack.

This is an extended metaphor. Term *A* is clearly the BBC's plans and term *B* is one of glass blowing, but it is extended or developed. Let's try and identify the words which extend or develop the metaphor — i.e., identify all the words to do with glass-blowing: *stretching glass*, *elaborately*, *thinly*, *strain*, *heat*, *flaw*, *crack*. Bragg is clearly suggesting that the glass blowing has not been a success because the glass (the BBC's resources) has been stretched so elaborately and thinly that the resultant strain is too great; he is also suggesting that the flaw in the glass (the lack of resources and the BBC's over-ambition) is so great that the heat (the competition from other television channels) is enough to cause an almighty crack (the breakdown of the BBC).

Is this metaphor effective? To answer this question, if you remember, we have first of all to establish if the metaphor is appropriate. It would appear from the explanation that it is: the *B* term (the glass-blowing image) seems to make clear Bragg's argument about the BBC's over-ambitious plans combined with its lack of resources. The metaphor, then, is appropriate, therefore effective. You could also add that it is highly striking and original.

But the wonderful thing about English is that there is no right answer. Remember what I said earlier in this book about the importance of the effect on you — your personal reaction. I think that this metaphor, however clever it might appear, is over-worked and flawed. Indeed, you could apply the metaphor to Bragg's own writing —

> like stretching the metaphor more and more elaborately, more and more thinly until the strain becomes unbearable. The heat of the writing and the flaw in the argument brings about the most almighty crack.

It is not only that his metaphor is too contrived, it is also inconsistent. The strain, according to the image, is caused by the glass (the BBC's resources — staff, equipment, money) being over-stretched by ambition (it is stretched elaborately) and by lack of money (it is stretched thinly). So far so good. But in the next sentence he changes direction: he moves from talking about the strain to talking about a crack brought about by a flaw in the glass. The flaw mentioned in this second sentence has nothing to do with the strain that he has been talking about in the first. In this second sentence, the crack is brought about by the *flaw*, not the strain, but the flaw, we learn, is the ambition, yet he has already identified the ambition in the first sentence as the elaborate *stretching* of the glass not the flaw in it. See what I mean by inconsistent?

You can argue the effectiveness of this metaphor either way: undoubtedly it is clever and memorable, yet there is a flaw in the metaphor that prevents it, for me, being entirely successful.

Isn't English wonderful? You can't really argue about two plus two equalling four, but you can argue about the effectiveness of metaphors!

Bear with me while we try another one. The following extract comes from a past Interpretation paper!

> The awakening was strange. I think I must have been aware of the noise of people entering the house, one of those slow fuses of sound that sputteringly traverses the unconscious until it ignites into wakening. My consciousness and the room came into the light together. My eyes were bruised with brightness. What I saw seems in retrospect to have had the shiningness of newly minted coins, all stamped unmistakably as genuine, pure metal, the undepreciable currency of my life.

The following question was set:

> *Choose one of the extended images contained in this paragraph and show how effective you find it in describing the boy's awakening.*

There are two extended images — or metaphors — in this paragraph: the one concerning the fuse and the other concerning the newly minted coins. Note that although the sentence *My eyes were bruised with brightness* is also a metaphor (his eyes were not literally *bruised*), it is not extended, therefore you cannot use it in your answer.

Let us examine the words that extend the first metaphor: *slow fuse of sound*, *sputteringly*, *ignites*. Now we have to establish if this metaphor is appropriate by asking the question: *how* did the boy awaken? He awoke slowly, hesitatingly, suddenly becoming aware of being awake. Is the metaphor, then, appropriate? The fuse image captures the slowness of the awakening (*slow fuse*), the fact that he awakens hesitantly (*sputteringly*), and the fact that he is suddenly wide awake (*ignites*). There is the idea of almost slowly exploding into consciousness. The metaphor is therefore very effective.

The second metaphor is extended by words such as *shiningness, newly minted, stamped, genuine, pure metal, undepreciable currency*. Ask yourself if this image is appropriate in describing what the boy saw when he woke up. He tells us that it was as though he had come into the light and everything was bright. We have already been told earlier in the extract that it was his parents that he saw when he woke up. The coin image captures much of that idea: his parents appear as shiny as newly minted coins, stamped as genuine, the pure metal and undepreciable currency of life. The metaphor certainly explains the value of the experience (*coins, pure metal*), the originality and untarnished nature of the experience (*newly minted*), though I am less certain of the idea of *undepreciable currency* since all currencies of which I have experience depreciate in value through time.

I have spent much time in dealing with the evaluation of metaphors since that is an important aspect of textual analysis.

CHAPTER ELEVEN

A Worked Example (1)

In this chapter, we shall attempt a textual analysis of the following poem by Robert Frost, using the techniques which you have learned from this book.

First of all, read the poem a couple of times very carefully:

Stopping by Woods on a Snowy Evening	
Whose woods these are I think I know.	*a*
His house is in the village though;	*a*
He will not see me stopping here	*b*
To watch his woods fill up with snow.	*a*
My little horse must think it queer	*b*
To stop without a farmhouse near	*b*
Between the woods and frozen lake	*c*
The darkest evening of the year.	*b*
He gives his harness bells a shake	*c*
To ask if there is some mistake.	*c*
The only other sound's the sweep	*d*
Of easy wind and downy flake.	*c*
The woods are lovely, dark and deep,	*d*
But I have promises to keep,	*d*
And miles to go before I sleep,	*d*
And miles to go before I sleep.	*d*
	Robert Frost

As always, let's start by looking at structure. The poem seems at first glance to be very simple — four stanzas, regular rhythm, and a rhyme scheme. But look closely at the rhyme scheme, which I have set out above for you. At first, the rhyme scheme seems straightforward, but the more you look at it, the more unusual and complex it appears. The first, second, and fourth lines in the first three stanzas all rhyme, while, in each of stanzas 2 and 3, the first, second, and fourth lines rhyme with the third line of the previous stanza. In the stanza 4, all four lines rhyme and, indeed, the third and fourth lines end in the same word.

All this creates a very tight effect, giving the poem a coherence which holds together ideas that are not obviously connected. What are the ideas? Think of our question *(a)*: *What is the poem about?* The poet, undertaking a long journey, has stopped by some woods to watch them fill up with snow and reflect on aspects of his own life. The rhyme scheme of the first stanza draws attention to the snow, and we begin to see it symbolically. Snow reminds us of winter, and, in turn, winter makes us think of — symbolises — death. Is the poem, then, about death? If it is, it cannot be a fearful or violent death since the line *To watch his woods fill up with snow* does not suggest a vicious, frightening snowstorm, but a gentle, gradual falling of snow and therefore a gentle, even gradual, death. The fact that the poet uses the words "to watch" further suggests something almost fascinating but not terrifying.

But I said that the rhyme links the ideas. If we follow through our notion that the poem is about death, what other ideas does the rhyme link it to? The rhyme links the "here" in line 3 of the first stanza with the second stanza and, in particular, *The darkest evening of the year.* The idea suggested by that line is mid-winter (death) and combined with the idea that it is the *darkest* evening further suggests death. There is also a supernatural connotation to the idea of the winter solstice, a feeling that there are powerful forces unleashed at that time, and the poet and his horse are in the midst of nature.

The last line of stanza 3 ends on "flake", another reminder of snow, but also of gentleness, even beauty. Indeed the rhyme draws attention to many images of gentleness and beauty throughout the poem: he refers to his *little horse*, even to the anthropomorphic notion that his horse might *think it queer*, the *frozen lake*, to the horse giving *his harness bells a shake*, to the only sound *being the sweep / Of easy wind*, to *downy flake*. In the first line of stanza 4, he actually refers to the woods being *lovely*, while using the adjectives *dark* and *deep*. *Dark* suggests mystery, even death, while *deep*, also suggesting mystery, further suggests something almost reflective, something that lies beyond our understanding. There is no threat in this poem, only beautiful images of winter and maybe therefore of death.

You also have to note the part that sound plays in the poem: without exception, the last word of each line contains a long vowel sound, contributing to the gentle effect, but adding a slow-moving, unhurried, almost wistful effect. Remember what we said about the effect of long vowel sounds, especially when combined with soft consonants such as *kn, th, h, sn*, etcetera.

Note that we have discussed structure, rhyme, word choice, sound, and now mood. The mood of the poem is one of gentle reflection, maybe even with a touch of regret.

Yet there are puzzling aspects to the poem. The poet says in the first line: *Whose woods these are I think I know.* Note the unusual structure of the line (and the sentence) where the normal word order — *I think I know whose woods these are* — has been reversed to draw attention to the *I know*. Yet whoever owns these woods lives in the village and will not see the poet stopping. Who is *he*? What is his relationship to the poet? What would he do if he could see the poet stopping — prevent him? Tell him to get a move on? Get him to return to the village? The place is empty — the world is empty — not even a farmhouse nearby.

Let's look again at the last stanza. He positions, at the very beginning of the second line, the word *but*, which, as you know, signals a change in direction, an exception to what the poet has been talking about. The woods fascinate him, and the suggestion is that he would continue to watch, *but* he cannot because he has promises to keep. What promises? To whom? Himself? The person referred to in stanza 1? Furthermore, by using the word

And, he links the idea of having promises to keep with the idea that he has miles to go before he sleeps.

> But I have promises to keep,
> And miles to go before I sleep,
> And miles to go before I sleep.

Not only does he link the idea of the journey to promise-keeping, but he repeats the line *And miles to go before I sleep*, thus drawing attention to its significance and also to its importance. The fact that he positions the lines right at the end of the poem further draws attention to them. Moreover, so far we have not said anything much about rhythm; if you read the whole of this stanza aloud, you will hear that the rhythm is the rhythm of everyday speech, it's an ordinary, everyday rhythm, not at all poetic, apart from the repetition of the line. The ordinariness of the rhythm and the link between the journey and promise-keeping combine to create a deceptively simple stanza, the meaning of which only slowly emerges. Does *before I sleep* refer to death, the poet's death? And does that mean that he has made promises to someone that he has to fulfil before he dies? Or is he merely anticipating death? Welcoming it as something of which one must not be afraid, but as something gentle, fascinating, but not yet for him because he has promises to keep?

So far, we have discussed verse and sentence structure, rhyme, sound, word choice, rhythm — and I have to stress that these techniques all contribute to or support meaning. That is, they support what the poem is about.

Often, in textual analysis, you will be asked to look again at the title of a poem in the light of having studied the text, and in the case of *Stopping by Woods on a Snowy Evening* the title takes on more significance after we have fully understood the poem. Frost's use of the present participle, *Stopping*, for example, suggests a casual, impermanent action, as though the stop is brief, but it is only after we have studied the poem that we fully realise that that is precisely what happens — he stops briefly and then continues his journey. We realise that the stopping and the continuing are symbolic of something more universal. But also, the word *evening* takes on greater significance after having studied the poem since evening, too, can be symbolic of the end of life just as evening is the end of the day. The word *snowy* creates the gentle impression that we have talked about. This is not a violent and threatening snow-storm, but something beautiful, almost mesmerising.

The title, at first glance, appears incidental, as though Frost was not that concerned about a title. Yet once you have read the poem, you only then realise that this title is not incidental but highly significant in that it encapsulates all that the poem is about.

Finally, I have to stress again that whatever interpretation the reader makes of the poem is what matters. You may well argue that this is not a poem about death but about, say, relationships — the relationship of the man to his horse or to the person who owns the woods or to the person to whom he made the promises. That is perfectly acceptable, as long as you can justify your claim with reference to the text. Some people may well argue that all that matters is what Frost *meant* by the poem, but, as I hope I have made clear, we don't know what Frost meant and in any case it doesn't matter, it's what the reader makes of a text, what the reader sees in it, that counts.

CHAPTER TWELVE

A Worked Example (2)

In this chapter, we shall examine — analyse — a final piece of text, again a poem by Robert Frost:

> *The Road Not Taken*
>
> Two roads diverged in a yellow wood,
> And sorry I could not travel both
> And be one traveller, long I stood
> And looked down one as far as I could
> To where it bent in the undergrowth;
>
> Then took the other, as just as fair,
> And having perhaps the better claim,
> Because it was grassy and wanted wear;
> Though as for that the passing there
> Had worn them really about the same,
>
> And both that morning equally lay
> In leaves no step had trodden black.
> Oh, I kept the first for another day!
> Yet knowing how way leads on to way,
> I doubted if I should ever come back.
>
> I shall be telling this with a sigh
> Somewhere ages and ages hence:
> Two roads diverged in a wood, and I —
> I took the one less travelled by,
> And that has made all the difference.
>
> *Robert Frost*

This time I would like you to do most of the work yourself in analysing the text, though I shall prompt you as we go along. You should use all that you have already learned to help you in your analysis. Remember the first of our three questions: *What is the poem about?* I think it helps, on this occasion, to begin with the situation. The poem is called *The Road Not Taken* and obviously the word "not" is highly significant. It would appear that the poem is about someone (the poet or persona — the character in the poem) who wants to travel through woods and is faced with a choice of paths. He would like to travel both paths but recognises that he can't and chooses the one less travelled by. By examining the situation we begin to get an idea of what the poem is about.

What effects does it have on me? Let's examine the mood because that will help us arrive at an answer to this question about effect. What is the mood? We have, as always, to analyse word choice: words and phrases such as *And sorry, long I stood*, and *I doubted* suggest a contemplative, thoughtful, almost wistful mood. The author, faced with this choice, seems not to be in a hurry.

We need, however, to examine the word choice in the lines:

> *Yet knowing how way leads on to way,*
> *I doubted if I should ever come back.*

The change from the idea of paths to the use of the word *way* and his acknowledgement that way often leads on to way makes us feel that these are not just literal paths through this wood. We go on to recognise that maybe there is a bit more to the idea of paths in a wood than merely getting physically from one place to another. We realise, then, that the wood is a metaphor — the poem may have been prompted by actual paths through an actual wood, but nevertheless there is the suggestion that the paths through the wood may have a figurative meaning — they may, for example, be paths through life. The author (or persona), then, sees himself as having a choice in life.

In the light of that metaphor, let's now look again at the language of the poem:

> *Two roads diverged in a yellow wood,*
> *And sorry I could not travel both*

What does the word "diverged" suggest? Note that he does not state that the roads separated or were separate — they diverged, therefore they are, to begin with, somehow connected. Is there anything else in the poem that suggests that the roads are connected? Look at the line at the end of verse two and the line at the beginning of verse three:

> *Though as for that the passing there*
> *Had worn them really about the same,*
>
> *And both that morning equally lay*
> *In leaves no step had trodden black.*

The roads are very similar: *(a)* both have been equally travelled on and are worn to the same level, though *(b)* neither has been worn down that much. From the quotation above, which words / phrases support the two points I have made about the roads?

Interestingly, the use of the word *that* the phrase *that morning* suggests a very specific point in time, as though he was suddenly presented one morning with this choice. And, furthermore, the line *In leaves no step had trodden black*, suggests, by the use of the phrase *no step had trodden black* that, though there had been traffic using the paths, nevertheless an insufficient number of people had used the paths to cause them any damage or destruction. These are unspoiled paths. The metaphorical suggestion is, then, that the two choices are for a career (or lifestyle or whatever) that is uncommon or unconventional. Not many people have been there.

Clearly, he wants to know where at least one of the roads leads to:

> *And looked down one as far as I could*

But he cannot quite see:

> *To where it bent in the undergrowth;*

What do you think the "undergrowth" refers to? What might it represent at a metaphorical level?

He then takes the other. The only difference with the one he chooses is that it perhaps is a little less worn, though later on he tells us that they were both worn about the same. What does that say about the choice that lies before him? If, then, by "roads" he means paths through life, and given what we have just said about the nature of the choice, what kind of choices might we deduce he means? I have already suggested career or lifestyle, but what else might the choices be?

How have these effects been achieved? We need to analyse the various techniques which Frost has employed. We have already looked at word choice, which is how we came to the conclusion that the poem is metaphorical. But let's go on to examine the rhyme scheme. Remember how to do that using *a, b,* and *c*? What do you notice? Is the rhyme scheme tight? Has it a complexity that matches the complexity of the thought? One clue: what do you think is the effect of rhyming the second and last lines of each verse?

And what about rhythm? In *The Road Not Taken*, it is obviously very regular — in a sense poetic. Look at the third line of the first verse where the break in the line after "traveller" creates a pause before "long I stood", a very poetic effect which draws attention to the words "long I stood". The poetic rhythm of the poem continues until the last verse, where the last line, by contrast, becomes almost conversational in feel, thus highlighting the meaning. Not only that, but the rhythm, close to that of conversation or everyday speech, suggests understatement, a device which draws our attention to meaning: his choice in lifestyle (or whatever) has had a dramatic — and long-lasting — effect on him. The whole point of the poem, then, is made clear in the last line because of these techniques: that choosing to take the unconventional route in life can make a huge difference to a person.

The more you analyse the poem — any poem — the more of its meaning emerges. But textual analysis is not some arcane art that only the initiated can understand or grasp: it is a fairly precise procedure, and I trust that the framework of the three questions — *What is the poem about? What effects does it have on me? How have the effects been achieved?* — will help you enormously in tackling texts. Although the procedure is precise, we are not, of course, dealing with an exact science. Begin with question *(a)* — *What is the text about?* — but realise that the answer will be fairly superficial at first, and only after you have tackled the next two questions will the full theme of the poem — or text — emerge. Once you have grasped the full theme, will more and more effects become clearer, and in turn more and more of the techniques will be revealed.

It is all worth it in the end because you will understand, and therefore appreciate, more and more of the text being analysed.

Before we conclude, however, let's have a look at the kind of questions, relating to this particular poem, that you might be asked in the Textual Analysis part of the paper. As I said previously, you might be asked a question about situation and / or mood, and this poem lends itself to such a question:

(a) By close examination of word choice, say what the situation is in this poem and what mood is evoked. (4 marks)

Other questions might be as follows. Try answering them yourself:

(b) There is a break or pause (often referred to as a caesura) in the middle of line 3. Comment as fully as you can on the effect of this pause. (2 marks)

(c) Comment on the ways in which the poet uses sound to enhance the mood in the first verse and in the last verse. (4 marks)

(d) At which point in the poem did you realise the importance of the metaphor? Explain exactly how you reached that conclusion. (4 marks)

(e) In what ways does the author establish the connection and the contrast between the two "paths" or "ways"? (6 marks)

(f) Comment as fully as you can on the structure of the first sentence of the poem. (4 marks)

(g) How does the use of rhyme contribute to and / or reinforce the overall effect of the poem? (2 marks)

(h) How effective is the last line as a conclusion to the whole poem? (4 marks)

I trust that, by now, these questions did not pose too much of a problem! And I also trust that you are much less frightened by the prospect of answering questions in Textual Analysis.

CONCLUSION

I have always felt that the only approach to the understanding of literature is by means of textual analysis. For too long, literature has been "taught": students have been given screeds of notes to be learned by heart and then reproduced in an examination. Too many teachers have told too many generations of young people what to think, what any given play, poem, or novel is about. Too many young people have consequently failed to recognise or even understand that it is what they think that matters, that theme is not embedded in the text (or in a teacher's head) but is a function of the reader and the reading process, that there is no "right" answer, only opinion — as long as the opinion is justified by close reference to the text.

When you watch a film or a video, you don't have to be told what it is about: you know yourself. You know the bits you like and the bits you don't like, the bits that are effective — have you on the edge of your seat or have you laughing or have you crying or feeling sad. You know when (and why) you identify with one of the characters or hate him or feel frightened by him. You know what the mood or atmosphere is and, with a little thought, you know how that mood or atmosphere has been created — what devices the director has used to make you feel creepy or scared or happy.

It should be the same with literature. When you read a novel or a poem or see a play, you should not — do not — really have to be told what it is about. By now you know from Chapter One that there are really only three themes — birth, marriage and death — and that they should guide you in determining what a given text is about. The study of English literature should not be an arid, stultifying business of being told what to think, but ought to be challenging and rewarding. But to study it effectively, you require skills in order to understand the various techniques used by writers. That way you will derive much enjoyment from the text.

Reading, like everything else, is a skill — one which must be learned, developed, and practised. This book, I trust, should have added to the skills that you already possess so that you are in a better position to analyse a text and thereby understand and appreciate it. What I hope more than anything is that you realise by now that being able to analyse, understand, and appreciate a text is not a series of hoops to be jumped through for the sake of exam success but is an essential aspect of being able to come to terms with the number of images — from television, newspapers, advertising, the Internet — with which we are increasingly surrounded. Since so many of these images are linguistic, the ability to analyse a text is of vital importance.

Happy, and fruitful, reading.

ACKNOWLEDGEMENTS

We hereby acknowledge the use of copyright material in this book
and are grateful to those for granting this permission.

PASSING WISDOM OF BIRDS
from *Crossing Open Ground*
by Barry Lopez
Reprinted by permission of the publishers Macmillan, London, UK.

A HANGING
by George Orwell
(Copyright © George Orwell 1931)
Reprinted by permission of Bill Hamilton as the
Literary Executor of the Estate of the Late Sonia Brownell Orwell
and the publisher Secker & Warburg Ltd.

THE CASTLE
from *Collected Poems*
by Edwin Muir.
Reprinted by permission of the publishers Faber & Faber Ltd.

THE ONLY CHILD
from *A Child of the Tyne*
by James Kirkup
Reprinted by permission of the publishers Edwin Mellen Press Ltd.

STOPPING BY WOODS ON A SNOWY EVENING
from *The Poetry of Robert Frost*
by Robert Frost
Edited by Edward Connery Lathem,
the Estate of Robert Frost and Jonathan Cape as publisher.
Used by permission of The Random House Group Limited.

THE ROAD NOT TAKEN
from *The Poetry of Robert Frost*
by Robert Frost
Edited by Edward Connery Lathem,
the Estate of Robert Frost and Jonathan Cape as publisher.
Used by permission of The Random House Group Limited.

Extract from *The Manor Farm*
by Edward Thomas published by Faber & Faber Ltd.

Extract from *The Pearl*
by John Steinbeck published by Heinneman Publishers

Extract from *Preludes*
by T.S. Eliot published by Faber & Faber Ltd.

Extract from *Dulce et Decorum Ests*
by Wilfred Owen published by Chatto & Windus Ltd.